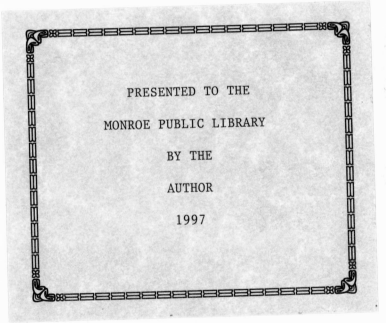

You Can Make Your Fortune!

LET HEAVEN
MAKE YOUR
FORTUNE

TOSHU FUKAMI

Tachibana Shuppan

CONTENTS

Fukuri Zao Gongen

Promoter of Good Fortune for Subsidiary Businesses

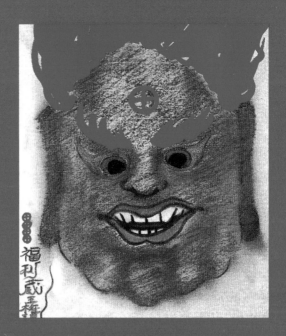

- **Seichu Bishamonten**—Posseses enormous power based on abandonment of evil for good – God of monetary fortune of the most stupendous kind. The god for those who seek success in their main buisiness.

- **Fukuri Zao Gongen**—God who is a great custodian of various forms of earthly wisdom. (For detailed explanation, see Chapter 2)

- **The Out Evil/In Virtue Divine World Logo**—Incorporates five kinds of virtue ; indispensable logo for attracting good fortune.

1) Acumen in decision making, 2) Choosing the right job, 3) Solving problems, 4) Boosting vitality, 5) Ability to take advantage of the arrival of good fortune

Note that pendant-style objects featuring the logo (available from Cosmomate) have the inherent power to ward off traffic accidents and other misfortunes.

For futher information contact **Worldmate** in Shizuoka :

☎ (0558) 76-1060

Seichu Bishamonten

*Promoter of Good
Fortune for Main
Businesses*

**The Out Evil/In Virtue
Divine World Logo**

*Guarantees Remarkable
Success in Monetary
Affairs*

PROLOGUE

Right Thinking Will Make Your Dreams Come True

Everyone Has His Share of Chances

Don't Keep Company With the "God of Poverty"

No one wants to be poor or to live a life of misfortune. Nevertheless, the world is filled with people, who no matter how hard they may try cannot shake the "God of Poverty" from their back and consequently continue to suffer.

The fact is that the way things are in this world without money nothing is possible.

Want to catch a movie, enjoy a good meal, buy some fashionable clothes or go out on a date? None of these things are possible unless you have the necessary funds.

On the other hand, if you have the financial wherewithal, you can see most of your dreams come true. You can ride about town in a Mercedes-Benz, live in a luxury condominium, dress in famous brand-name clothes and enjoy delicious French food at a first-class restaurant whenever you so choose to.

Be that as it may, there is no guarantee that even if you are loaded with money you will be able to enjoy true happiness. Many a lonely millionaire lives a cheerless existence in his mansion, while some of the residents of filthy, cramped tenement apartments are enjoying their lives to the fullest. In other words, whether or not a person has a good deal of money does not in itself tell us whether or not he or she is going to be happy or miserable.

Still, looking at the matter logically, we must frankly admit that anyone who declares to the world "I don't need money" is lying.

Clearly this is a case of: It is better to have than have not, and it is better to have as much as you can than to have just a little.

To put it bluntly, although there is no direct connection between whether a person does or does not have money and the degree of happiness or unhappiness in his or her heart, there is a very profound indirect connection. As the Japanese proverb *It is hard for an empty sack to stand straight* makes clear, when people are down on their luck, the impact of their poverty strikes all the way into their hearts.

Then there is another proverb *Poverty dulls the wits* that has long served as a warning. However, it should be borne in mind that the opposite is also frequently true. The richer people are, the more tight-fisted they often become. That is exactly the reason why they could accumulate so much wealth in the first place.

I am firmly convinced that our souls must be fulfilled and our pocketbooks in sufficiently good shape if we are to really enjoy our lives. The reason is that only if we are in such a condition can we also be guaranteed a happy existence when we return to the realm of the spirits.

It must be admitted, however, that some people just cannot get their just rewards and never seem able to escape the hell of poverty. Why should that be? Or to put it another way: Why is it that some people seem to go from one success to the next in this world and pile up wealth without hardly trying? Isn't that patently unfair? Can there really be any gods or Buddhas if such a patently unfair situation is allowed to exist?

Such thoughts undoubtedly run through the minds of many people when they see the way things are in life.

Even though we frequently say that there are many things in life more important than money, the fact is that with the exception of

3

life itself, money is probably the most important thing around. Well then, how do you go about getting your hands on this precious commodity?

People naturally believe that if they put out the required effort, pay their dues so to speak, then they should approach as close to true happiness as everyone else who has done the same. In other words, they believe it their just due or right to enjoy good fortune when it comes to money. When after working, slaving and sweating, they think they have grabbed the brass ring, but instead discover they are holding that old "God of Poverty," some people cannot understand why they should be alive at all.

It would seem only just and fitting that he who puts out an ounce of effort should be rewarded with its equivalent in monetary success. But true good fortune when it comes to money is really like getting back the equivalent of one ounce of effort ten times over. In such a case you can enjoy personal happiness and also help make many other people happy. The purpose of this book is to explain exactly how you can gain such ten-fold happiness.

In addition to my activities as a spiritualist, I operate several private companies. So I am naturally quite busy. Sometimes I feel that it is impossible for my single self to do everything I need to do. So I have come to realize that I need to follow a two-pronged strategy: eliminating all waste of time and relying on the kind of wisdom that *kills three birds with one stone*, so to speak, while also developing the talents of my subordinates so that they can help me bear the load. During my various activities, I try to keep this strategy firmly in mind.

When it comes to the question of good fortune in money matters, I look at things from this same perspective of necessity and responsibility, and it has become the basis of the know-how I have managed to acquire in this sphere. I also like to think of these things as benefits resulting from my attempts to follow, as well as I am able, the precepts of a way of life that gives thought to both the gods and humankind.

In other words, conformance to this path requires heeding the wishes of the gods and executing as best we can our mission as human beings. So the know-how I am speaking of really amounts to trying to be as one with the gods and Buddhas.

Some of my readers undoubtedly assume that because I am an expert on the spirit world, I must have a special knack for getting the gods to listen to me when I ask for divine assistance.

But I should like to make absolutely clear at this point that when it comes to managing a business or creating good luck with money, well-couched appeals to the gods are in themselves just not enough. If you do not possess drive, sincerity and a sense of devotion, then it does not matter one iota how fine your appeals to the gods may be. They will go unnoticed in the spirit world.

Be that as it may, in this book I will touch upon some of my experiences in the field of business and I hope that my recounting them will help to make it perfectly clear that with a small degree of effort you too can achieve good fortune in money matters and by the use of proper, proven prayers you can tap sources of power outside yourself to boost your capabilities and display your own good fortune regarding money. I hope to tell you exactly how to accomplish these things in the pages that follow.

Bear in mind, however, that this book is not solely intended to give you the know-how required so that you can be a success in this world. More importantly I, Toshu Fukami, will explain from the perspective of the spirit world how success is to be achieved, money made and that money used to attain happiness in both your present and future lives.

I also hope to show you how by developing the right frame of mind and making the required effort you can win over your protective spirits and the gods of the spiritual world to your side, attract good fortune in monetary and other facets of life to your person and totally root out any surviving seeds of misfortune. If you study the contents of this book thoroughly and put its lessons to work in your daily life, I guarantee that you will achieve these results in your own daily life.

As I explained in my earlier book *Lucky Fortune,* good luck is not something that is bestowed on us from above. Rather it is something we the living bring to ourselves and at the same time should actively search out. The same thing holds true for the theme of this book – good luck in money affairs. It will never do for us to just sit there with our arms folded, waiting. We have to get up, get out and grab that good luck for ourselves.

But be forewarned. There are perils involved if you just haphazardly rush around. As I will explain in detail later, the powerful evil spirits who inhabit the Makai or hells are determined to drag you down to the nether regions with them. And one of the ploys they will use in this quest is the desire of human beings for wealth.

So from the perspective of your spiritual fate, as well as your life in this physical world, the first thing to bear in mind is that you must use correct means when courting good fortune. If you neglect or refuse to do so, then you are letting yourself in for some unpleasant surprises when you return to the spirit world. And you will also bring misfortune to those near and dear to you, including your children and grandchildren.

Don't Mess With the Makai

There are any number of cases in which a family prospers during one generation. But it is rare to find a family that sustains this prosperity over three generations. The first generation slaves and endures terrible hardships to accumulate wealth. But the second generation does well enough to preserve what it has received and the third generation more often than not forgets the efforts of the grandparents and squanders the wealth that cost them so much hard work and sweat. That is the general pattern at least.

In Japan we have a famous proverb that well sums up this phenomenon. It could be translated as: *A thrifty grandfather, a spendthrift grandson* or *Clogs to clogs in three generations*. There is a tendency to blame this situation on the alleged reckless extravagance of sons and grandsons or the way the tax system is fixed to make sure that wealth cannot be passed down as far as the third generation. But that assessment is proved untrue if you look at things from the perspective of the spirit world. The real reason or predisposing factor that accounts for the fact that the wealth acquired by the first generation is usually dissipated by the third generation is rooted in the questionable ways in which the money was accumulated by the first generation to begin with.

Honestly speaking, wealth that is acquired at the expense of creating grudges or unhappiness among other people is almost invariably destined to disappear without a trace by the time of the third generation simply because it reeks of the malice it has created in others. Furthermore, in such a situation, no matter how rich a person may become, he or she will never think in a bright, healthy fashion. Such a person will not only not know love, he or she will never experience the pure happiness of non-attachment to material things. In addition, the evil deeds committed in a person's former existence, which are objectively manifested as suffering forced on others, and his or her corrupt way of thinking guarantee banishment to some hell in the afterlife.

Consequently, riches acquired at the cost of unhappiness for others are not the real thing at all. No doubt many of my readers are saying to themselves at this point, "That's perfectly O.K. I just want to be rich!" But I say to you, "Hold on and reconsider."

It may be true that such tactics can make you money, which means that you will be able to enjoy a luxurious life. But that lifestyle can last at the utmost only 50 or 60 years. Then what's going to happen when this life is over and done with? Your life in the spirit world still awaits you. And so too will a hell that will symbolically embody all the feelings of bitterness and all the curses that those whom you have wronged are directing at you.

"You never thought of anyone but yourself. All our suffering and sorrows didn't mean a thing to you. Damn you....you bastard...."

"Because of you I am a slave to bitter memories. Now you're going to suffer just like I have...."

Even as you are berated by your vengeful victims, you will sink into the pit of suffering that will contort your body and soul. You will be constantly tormented by these apparitions of the living while you are still on earth, and after you die and go to this hell you will find waiting punishments especially designed so that you will suffer in the kinds of ways that you made the innocent suffer while you were alive. In other words, you will reap what you have sown. What is more, you will have to remain in this hell for a minimum of 300 to 400 years.

On top of that, these punishments of hell will also be visited upon your living children and grandchildren.

What is happening here is that your individual debt that has to be paid off in the spirit world is partly parceled out to your kin without your kin even being aware of it. This entire debt has to be wiped out. In this fashion, rich families sink into poverty and the descendants of those who gained their wealth through immoral means have to drink deeply from the cup of cruel poverty. So the man who made his fortune through reliance on evil forces compels his children and grandchildren to pay the price needed to wipe his slate of sin clean. In other words, it is only through their suffering that little by little their ancestor who suffers in hell can be saved.

There are many cases of third generation heirs in rich families who are addicted to the worst forms of gambling, or who go way overboard in regards to drink and sex. We also hear of the kind of people pleasers who end up acquiring "friends" who sponge off them mercilessly. In such ways the wealth of their parents is dissipated. Appraising such behavior by human standards, we have to say that it is despicably evil. But, if evaluated in a slightly different way, in many cases these people actually seem paragons of piety towards their grandparents.

The reason is that in the spirit world money that has been acquired in improper ways is transformed into the most vile filth that has an overpowering stench. And property takes the form of heavy black iron bars that weigh down on the damned. Since they naturally want to do anything possible to escape this suffering, they lay a curse on the wealth that has been passed on to their grandchildren. It is only when these ill-gotten riches have been completely used up that they can attain complete peace of mind. Thus, there is a spiritual reason why some people cannot control their dissipation.

For that reason, it is not for us to judge any of our fellows, since only the gods are capable of making an accurate assessment of the good and evil involved.

Be that as it may, it is not hard to find people of whom it is said, "Hard to believe, but his grandparents were loaded with money," or, "They used to be big in this town and people listened when they talked, but now as you can see they're really down on their luck."

However, such people should not moan about their lot. If they simply accept the fact that their poverty is a kind of living memorial to their ancestors, then they should feel somewhat better.

And even if you were born into such a family, refrain from complaining about or bearing a grudge against your ancestors. The fact is that people are basically reborn in conditions that correspond precisely to the balance of vice and virtue they established during their previous lives. By not grumbling about your present circumstances and progressing straight ahead by doing the best you can, you will be able to reduce the bad marks you have on your record from your previous lives and build up your own account of virtue. This becomes a kind of savings for your next life.

True Good Fortune Is Built Up Steadily

"I don't give a hoot, I want money now! Even if it means unhappiness for the other guy, I want to live in that mansion on the hill!"

You better avoid thinking like this or else I guarantee that this desire of yours for good fortune based on self-centered desire is going to backfire and cause you, the people around you and even your descendants untold grief.

Well then, what kind of desire for money is virtuous? It goes without saying that you have to be in the frame of mind where you wish the best for your neighbor as well as yourself. Forgive me if I sound a little preachy here, but if you really want to bring yourself good luck when it comes to money, then I advise you to pay careful attention to the "rules of the spiritual world" that I will outline below.

Remember from the outset that true good fortune is rooted in the world of the spirit. This is prosperity that results from good deeds. There is also "good fortune" of a sort to be found in the world of devils and evil spirits. But this variety is a double-edged sword that brings misfortune along with riches. Consequently, such good financial fortune from the realm of darkness ends up being merely temporary and phony.

If you want to be a beneficiary of the true good fortune with money that only comes from the spiritual world, then the paramount consideration becomes whether the desires of the spirits and gods match your own hopes. Here what I mean by the "desires of the spirits and gods" is, needless to say, happiness for all humankind including naturally yourself.

A selfish manner of thinking that has room only for your individual happiness is not in accordance with the ways of the spiritual world. Similarly, extreme self-sacrifice is also not desired by the spirits and gods. That is because the gods worry about saving the individual, that is you, first before saving the world. The first thing is to make sure that you yourself are happy. That is the true desire of the spirits and gods. That is why the desire to see fortune come to both yourself and others is so important.

There is another very important aspect to this double desire. Good fortune in money matters manifests itself in very concrete form. But most of it is realized through the people around you. Happiness is a feeling inside the heart of a person, and to a certain extent it can be transformed by that person. But good luck with money is a matter of dollars and yen, and all talk of good fortune is meaningless unless it materializes in the form of money and property.

A person whose wallet is flat empty but who nevertheless claims *My luck with money is fantastic* is simply talking nonsense. Unless your wallet is bulging with crisp bills, then you have no right to talk about your good fortune. So the thing to do is to treat the people around you in a way that will ensure that they will in turn bring you that good fortune that will fill your wallet and save you from spouting nonsense. The spirits and gods set people in action, who in turn set money in action.

But do you seriously think that if you look out purely for yourself and do not give a damn about the other fellow, then your neighbor is going to come rushing to you bearing heaps of good luck? And if you have such an attitude, then the guardian spirits who are always by your side will not dish up any of that luck either. But if you are the kind of person who other people and the guardian spirits alike would be glad to lend a helping hand to, then there is no question but that good luck with money will come to you almost automatically. The potency of the basic principle of wishing good luck for both yourself and others is clearly evidenced here as well.

Thus when the spiritual world sets things in motion, so that others become more than willing to help you out, your good luck will gradually grow and gain a life of its own. And naturally, unless something extraordinary happens, the dissipation of the wealth you have acquired by your children and grandchildren will never occur. Because your happiness has resulted from your merit, your family will be blessed with good fortune and you will have fortunate descendants, who if they also act in a virtuous manner will be able to further improve your family's prosperity.

Luck in Finishing Things

Many people seem to try and try and try, but never receive the just reward they deserve for their efforts. Although they sweat and give their everything without giving up, it seems that they always fall one step short of their final goal. You also hear many people complaining that they have had the winner's prize snatched right out of their hands by someone else.

The principle that your reward will inevitably be commensurate with your labor certainly holds true when it comes to your personal spiritual growth and inner world. But this rule does not hold true when it comes to money matters. Hard work does not necessarily guarantee that your business will prosper, your sales zoom upward and that you will make it big in the world. Many men struggle hard but still fail.

One reason is that every such businessman has many rivals who are also all trying their hardest. It might also be that the individual just does not have the luck needed to win.

Of course, there are individuals whose hard work does not bear the least bit of fruit no matter how much they might try, because they lack sufficient clarity of foresight, creativity or the ability to express themselves to and win the support of other people. Perhaps there is a gap between the amount or type of effort they can expend and what it takes to make it in the world. Whatever the reason, no matter how much these people try, they cannot seem to make the grade. Such people simply have no luck?

Well then, what do you have to do to gain luck?

Inner Honesty Is the Key to Getting Lucky

One important factor is whether or not your timing is right. Luck is something that is brought to you. Those who recognize and adroitly take advantage of chances for good fortune that are laid at their doorsteps are lucky. As a general principle though, those who can frankly and honestly assess what they see stand the best chance to take full advantage of lucky opportunities that come their way. Conversely, people who like to split hairs and refuse to budge from their own preconceived notions are likely to miss their chances.

The essential purpose of Zen meditation and other spiritual training is to cultivate a heart that will look at things with total honesty. The concept of *munen muso*, or a serene state of mind similar to a void free from all ideas and worldly thoughts, is totally different in Zen than it is in Yoga. Zen is always firmly rooted in daily life and it is basically training designed to eliminate evil thoughts that interfere with our ability to see things honestly. However, since an in-depth discussion of the differences between Zen and Yoga would be far from the theme of this book, I will avoid it here. But suffice it to say there are fundamental differences.

If you can come to view everything around you, as well as yourself and the people you associate with with total honesty, then you will be able to discern good from evil in your own mind and therefore will not miss opportunities presented to you. Here I am not referring just to good luck in monetary matters. The same thing holds true for good fortune on your job and in your love life and marriage. On the other hand, failure to achieve this ability naturally has an adverse impact on your daily life.

All of us have guardian spirits who hover around us and are constantly trying to tell us Heaven's will. Some ways in which they do so are through premonitions, hunches and dreams that later come true. However, people who do not possess the capability to see and feel honestly will not pay any attention to these messages from the "invisible voices" of Heaven.

Even though our guardian spirits are always there seeking to tell us of chances, by utilizing the opinions and advice of other people as their conduit, men who refuse to be completely honest with themselves look upon such opinions and advice as being nothing more than unwanted meddling. All they end up doing is simply alienating other people and making themselves persona non gratis with the Goddess of Good Fortune.

It is often said that you will not miss chances if you can control the ego and rid yourself of illusions. But what exactly do you need to do to get rid of the irksome ego and wipe out those old illusions in order to be in the position to take advantage of opportunities?

Sometimes even though you understand a given situation in your mind, you cannot clearly ascertain what course of action you should take because of these defects of character.

I advise all my readers to live your lives according to the maxims *Train yourself to look at things honestly, Speak to others with honesty* and *Candidly speak your mind when you pray to your guardian spirits.* By so living, you will be able to purge the ego, shatter illusions and take advantage of the chances being offered you. Also remember, Japan's gods prefer a determinedly positive attitude to negative warnings and prohibitions.

You have two men who give the same amount of effort and engage in the same kind of behavior. But one gradually gets ahead in the world, while the other forever remains lost in the crowd. This case clearly illustrates the difference between a man who has luck with him and one who does not. The gap becomes especially conspicuous when it comes to luck with money. Whether or not you become lucky depends on your ability to judge the timing of your moves. The lucky man is ready and waiting when Lady Luck arrives. Moreover, he is ready to give 110 percent when fortune smiles on him.

An example from baseball will make this readily apparent.

A batter who steps up to the plate with two outs in the bottom of the ninth with the bases loaded can already be said to be a very lucky man since his hit can win the game.

All he has to do is take advantage of the endless days of training that preceded this chance. And he knows that should he get a hit in this situation, he is sure to get a raise the next year. The same hit in such a fabulously fortunate situation will be worth far more than if it came after the game had already been decided. The difference is like day and night.

What is strange though is that some batters frequently find themselves in this kind of situation, although others almost never do. The former are the kind of guy of whom other players tend to think, "If he comes to bat, he's liable to blow the game wide open." No doubt the player's mental power has become manifested in the physical world. It might be that his batting average is roughly the same as that of other hitters, but he is known to all as a "guy who knows how to take advantage of chances." For that reason, good chances seem to just come his way.

When it comes to luck with money, things are pretty much the same. Everyone is offered opportunities in which if they will just make that little extra effort they can translate good fortune into actual success. If when a chance arrives a person is ready to give his all, then monetary luck will be his. On the other hand, if a person overlooks his chances, then even if he strives as hard as he can at other times, he is likely to only get a few "singles," which will be irrelevant when it comes to scoring runs or winning the game.

But the person who continues to take maximum advantage of the chances that come his way might very well end up winning his team a pennant or garnering a MVP award (or make a fortune if we are talking about monetary luck). And the man who is known for his good fortune with money will become like the clutch hitter who everybody turns to when the chips are down.

"I think if you discuss this business with so-and-so, it might prove worth your while." He knows what he's talking about, so why don't you get his opinion." People will flock to the door of such a man with the Midas touch.

The next questions that will probably spring to mind are: "How do I respond when my chance comes along, so that I really will be able to give 110 percent?" and "If I get my initial chance, how can I keep luck on my side?"

Those are the questions I would like to explore in the next section of the book.

CHAPTER 1

Happiness Results From Making and Spending Money the Right Way

Skills and Aptitudes Needed to Achieve Solid Good Luck With Money

Cleverness and Skill Are Two Totally Different Things

A man who is clever with his hands, the kind of jack-of-all-trades who is good at whatever he does, may superficially seem very much like a truly talented man. But actually the two are basically completely different.

The clever man is quick to learn the knack of doing something. His fingers are dexterous and he is able to perform tasks smoothly. But that by no stretch of the imagination means that he can be considered a professional. Such a person's skill will never advance beyond the level of a hobby or a special flair.

But the true man of talent has skills of an unquestionably professional level, which means that his techniques might be imitated but they can never be matched. So the public is eager to pay to enjoy these special talents. In other words, mere cleverness does not translate into money-making, but real skill does.

What then constitutes the knack for making money? People value money next to life itself. Money inspires trust and the ability to make it draws the praise and recognition of society. One of the people to whom I have taught the art of exorcism is a fellow named Kiminori Nanasawa. Incidentally, Nanasawa is an accomplished composer and lyricist, and I consider him my teacher in those regards. Ever since he graduated from Keio University, one of

Japan's top private institutions of higher learning, he has dedicated himself to music. Nanasawa has told me:

"The cases of any number of friends has convinced me that no matter how ungifted a guitarist may be, if he keeps working at it for ten years, I will guarantee that he can make it as a pro guitarist. Although such a person might not have many albums out, or have his songs on the hit charts, or otherwise be in the spotlight, he will be able to make a living out of the guitar. But most people can't stick out those ten long years that lay the groundwork."

Nanasawa explains that a person who has two or three years of playing the guitar under his belt should be able to copy other people's styles easily enough. But a guitarist who has really worked at his craft for a decade will have a certain indefinable something in his style that his less experienced imitators cannot capture. So no one will be able to ape it that easily. It is a talent that is his and his alone. That is why people will come knocking on his door offering him money to perform.

The life of a professional is a hard one. That is because the sponsors who decide whether what he has to offer is commercially valuable or not are going to be tough in their assessments. If an individual cannot rise to the occasion under their scrutiny and deliver the goods when the chips are down, so that the prospective sponsor will admit, "You really are good," then he does not deserve to be considered a pro. And lucky flukes do not count in this regard.

Take the comparative case of a designer who fully realizes the sense of value and needs of his clients and always manages to provide the highest quality designs by the deadline agreed upon, versus a person who merely has an interest in design and for that reason went to an art school. There will be considerable differences between the two when it comes to attitude and the diligence they show in their job every day.

21

Such differences are sure to be reflected in degrees of skill and competency. The first will be accustomed to always being under the gun, knowing that his customers expect the very best, and consequently will not accept any compromises when it comes to the pursuit of excellence. In other words, good fortune with money requires strong, well-tempered will power. In fact, it is a byproduct of the greater levels of skill that directly result from this tempering process.

We all know the expression, "A jack-of-all-trades and master of none." It should serve as a warning to people who only have cleverness to depend on. Instead of dabbling in this and that, it is important for such people to concentrate on one thing alone until they achieve great success, a process that should take a decade at the very least. So the multi-talented man would be well-advised to tackle one field at a time, allotting at least ten years for each, and in this way his skills in each will gradually mature to the level of a professional.

With that in mind, the first thing to do is to ascertain very clearly exactly what your talents and capabilities are and then to do your utmost to make sure that you do not get stuck at the level of mere cleverness. *Your accomplishments will benefit you for your entire lifetime*, would be a good expression to keep in mind. And in addition, if you can polish your skills to where they are perfected to a professional level, then you will have no need to fear going hungry. Capabilities that cannot be transmuted into financial power cannot be considered the real thing.

Self-Satisfaction in Work and Life

There are some people in this world who are so talented that they cannot help but provoke envy among others. Then again, there are people who can write beautifully, speak foreign languages fluently, have amazing memories and have wonderful personalities, but nevertheless live in tenements.

Such situations would seem to contradict the tenet I proposed earlier, namely that any abilities that cannot be used to your financial advantage are not the real thing. But the fact remains that many people who are loaded with what would normally be called talent often are far from wealthy. The reason is extremely simple.

In place of an overwhelming desire to get rich, such individuals set a higher priority on perfecting their own skills, so they do not attract good monetary fortune.

These people really deserve to be placed in a separate category, since they are not unhappy just because they have not been blessed with monetary success. They are convinced that the highest form of happiness is to polish their own skills and to keep seeking to raise them to a higher level. Such a pattern is not at all unusual for people who have come to feel that there are more important things in life than money. Some people I know who play *shogi* (Japanese chess) or perform *rakugo* comic monologues professionally certainly belong to this category.

But a person who is really talented will pass on wealth to his descendants, even if he does not live in the lap of luxury while he is alive. Take for example the writer who suffers throughout his entire lifetime in obscurity in order to leave stories of enduring value, but who unfortunately does not receive recognition until after his death. There have been many cases in which such a person's works

posthumously become famous and for that reason their children and grandchildren become rich through possession of the copyrights.

So as you can see, towering talent does not guarantee wealth. But when that talent is finally recognized, the flower of good monetary fortune is certain to bloom. Maybe we should say that it is precisely because such people do not run around in the pursuit of money during their lifetimes, but instead concentrate every ounce of their energy on thoroughly developing their capabilities to their fullest that they are able to leave behind works that came to be recognized by others after their death.

If you look at things in that way in life, things seem to work out right in the end.

There are also those people who give their hard-earned money to others less fortunate, and consequently willingly live in poverty themselves. Such individuals are eligible to enter the Third Heaven after their deaths.

Talent Is Heaven's Reward for a Virtuous Past Life

Where does talent come from in the first place? Generally speaking, we have the seeds of our talents in us when we are born. If the innate talent is not there, then no matter how much a person might like a given field, and no matter how hard he may work at it, he is not likely to leave many accomplishments behind in that area.

For example, the average boy dreams of becoming a professional baseball player when he grows up. But most never play ball beyond the junior high school level. Only a tiny fraction of these boys actually grow up to become pros. It might be especially obvious with baseball, but no matter what field you turn to you will find men and women who are giving their all, but who unfortunately simply do not have what it takes in that particular area.

Although some such people are likely to take offense, I advise that they would be wise to give up and pour their energy into a different job that better matches their skills.

Some people might object, "By talking like that, aren't you just discouraging initiative?" But please hear me out.

The way things are viewed from the vantage point of the spiritual world, a person's talents are largely dependent on the learning, morality and personal strengths acquired during his previous existences. By *previous existences* I naturally mean the entire period before a person was born into this present life.

But it would be wrong to conclude that the human being he is now is the exact same person he was prior to being born this time around. As I explained in my previous book *Lucky Fortune*, the *soul* from previous existences is to be found active in the deepest part of the brain or psyche, in other words in the person's subconscious.

For example, there is a famous cartoonist in Japan named Reiji Matsumoto, who in a previous existence was none other than the famous Han Dynasty Chinese historian Ssu-ma Ch'ien. Although Matsumoto and Ssu-ma are of course two completely different people with lives of their own, Ssu-ma's fervent interest in digging into history survives in Matsumoto's subconscious. So we might attribute the fascination that Matsumoto exhibits towards history to the subliminal influence of Ssu-ma's continuing consciousness.

There are any number of similar examples of famous people today who were also famous in their past lives. I can think for instance of a famous fashion model who in the past was Izumo no Okuni, the dancer who is regarded as the founder of kabuki. And there is the female novelist Mariko Hayashi, who in the past was the French lawyer, educator and literary man La Bruyere. In fact almost without exception someone who in this life exhibits some special talent has a very close connection to a person in a previous life, who was similarly gifted in the same field or a related one.

All of this is not by accident. The reason is that the consciousness surviving from a previous life encourages a person to try his or her hand at a given field. It is this little voice that nudges a person in a certain direction. Although it defies theory and logic, this factor is extremely important in determining how we act.

So if there is a certain subject for which you display a lot of affinity, which constantly sparks your interest and which you just plain like, and in which you can score high marks even if you do not study, then you can conclude that it was an area in which you exerted yourself very hard in your past lives and therefore were able to acquire a great deal of talent in. It follows therefore that if you try your best in that same field in this existence then you should be able to finish the work you began in your previous life and leave behind fantastic achievements before you are through.

So if you consider the perfection of your skills as a marathon race, then you already ran the equivalent of nearly half during your past lives and only have to complete the remainder this time around.

Three Forms of Merit

On the other hand, we can also say that during our present lifetime we are acquiring capital, in the form of talent, to draw on in our next life. So even though we may not get the breaks in this life, if we perfect ourselves to the limit, then when we are reborn in the next life, we are sure to be at the front of the crowd when it comes to ability. The Japanese people in general are not much given to thinking in such terms, but many Chinese and Koreans think this way all the time.

So many of them seek to acquire virtue, confident that seven generations later they will be reborn as persons whose fame will spread throughout the entire country. This is really thinking on a grand scale: getting ready now through the display of an incredible spirit of perseverance.

I have learned from their example, so now instead of just trying to acquire merit for my next life, I have tried to work out nothing less than a "20,000-year game plan for life." The premise of this is that if during a period of 20,000 years a person continues to try his or her hardest through various reincarnations, then I am convinced that he or she can surpass the Buddha or Jesus Christ in spirituality and Michelangelo or Da Vinci in native genius. In other words, I have faith that he who perseveres and who never wavers in his determination over the long haul will triumph in the end.

In any event, by formulating such a far-reaching life program, I can better strive to take full advantage of all the days remaining to me in this life. And besides I seriously doubt whether 20,000 years from now anyone will remember the above declaration or anything else I have written down in this book. So I can be of peace of mind on that score. But seriously, I do try every single day to work towards this goal, and perhaps in that sense I even outdo the Chinese.

Well, I must apologize for digressing from the main topic of the book.

There are three kinds of activities in this life that affect our future lives and our standing in the spirit world:

• academic learning

- artistic expression
- religious faith

The pursuit of learning is an expression of our inquisitiveness, our desire to improve our understanding, our inclination to digest what we have already learned and our willingness to work hard. The child who is said to have been *born with a good head* on his or her shoulders undoubtedly studied hard in previous lives.

By artistic expression I really mean what is commonly referred to as *good aesthetic sense*. Such a gift can manifest itself in several different ways – a good ear, a good eye for color or the general ability to appreciate things of beauty, and an acute sensitivity to the infinite beauty in nature.

And finally, we have faith. This is the inherent sensibility that causes our hands to come together without premeditation in the attitude of prayer when we see an image of the Buddha or the guardian deity Jizo. Here again, if our souls are devoid of artificiality and we are capable of directly experiencing the gods and Buddhas, we can no doubt attribute these things to our faith in previous lives.

The three factors mentioned above are attributes of a highly sensory world. This is none other than the world of the departed spirits. Perceptions here are those of eternity, an eternity that incorporates but transcends the spiritual world and future lives. We might even call it an intangible treasure. But it is useless to think of it as being like our material world, where if you go all out in your work for a week you can expect to make such and such amount in monetary reward. It is harder to get results here. You must perfect your sensibilities, while striving little bit by little bit to achieve your goals.

But it is precisely by cultivating these three qualities that we are able during our lives to collect *winnings*. A better way to put it might be that from the perspective of the treasures we are piling up in Heaven, our gains are worth far more than mountains of gold. These spiritual gains in fact far excel monetary fortune in their virtue. Looking at things from another angle, we might say that the accumulation of spiritual *profits* automatically opens the door that good fortune will enter through.

Accumulating *profits* in this way really means that we are expanding the capabilities of our souls, bodies and senses. At the same time, we are naturally increasing our stature in the spirit world and inducing the protective deities to work harder on our behalf. On top of that, once we die and enter the spirit world, we can continue to fill up our spiritual treasury. It does not matter one iota whether we are in the world of men or in the world of the spirits, our efforts to achieve spiritual perfection can continue unabated at any place or time.

Whether we care for this process or not, whether the whole thing seems like too much trouble – such considerations are irrelevant. There is nothing we can do about it one way or another. This necessity to build up spiritual *profits* is an immutable law of the spirit world.

It Is Never Too Late

Do you spend all your time loathing your present job, never seem to get the hang of it and make no effort to get ahead? Just remember, if you have no desire to grow as a human being, then you can hardly expect to have good luck when it comes to money.

The state of mind required to develop your talents and enjoy good fortune with money can be equated with a sense of resolution to acquire the three kinds of profit or merit that I referred to earlier. You might think of the spirit that encourages us to learn everything we need to know about our job as a type of academic learning and the willingness to try to get along as well as possible with our superiors and colleagues as a way of building up our faith. Likewise, efforts to refine our sensibilities are really a form of artistic expression.

These three factors are even in operation in the daily life of a housewife. Cooking is of course an art. Listening carefully to what her husband or mother-in-law say helps the homemaker to develop her sense of faith. And managing the family budget needless to say requires a woman to learn many new things. If you look at things in this fashion then it becomes perfectly obvious that all aspects of human life really reflect a drive to accumulate *profits* of this sort.

If we adopt such a positive attitude, then life becomes a real pleasure and our troubles start to melt away. We no longer find the trials of life so difficult and we no longer seek to shy away from the world. And nothing is better guaranteed to please our guardian spirits than such a no-holds-barred commitment to living. Adopt it and you will soon find yourself enjoying immense good fortune in money, family affairs, health and every other facet of your life.

On top of that, your efforts to live in such a positive fashion will naturally cause the latent talents within you, that you were never even aware of, to bloom and contribute actively to your further development.

If you become obsessed with gaining good luck with money, then your heart will fall prey to intoxication with the material. However, if you can step back and calmly judge what is really important in your life and what course of action you need to take, then you will discover naturally what you need to do.

Before jumping to the conclusion that you lack talent and luck when it comes to money and thereby succumbing to feelings of worthlessness and dissatisfaction, you should stop and once more review the circumstances of your daily life. It is essential that you estimate with all the honesty at your command how hard you have been working to build up merit in your life.

Never adopt the mistaken attitude that it is too late to start. Instead make up your mind to start this very day on increasing the merit within you. I can assure you that this is the real key to acquiring eternal good fortune with money.

I also hope that you will never flag in your desire to learn. By learning I mean not just acquired knowledge about the material world, but also an awareness of the profound truths of the spiritual world. You should also develop an appreciation stemming from the depths of your soul for things of beauty.

And even should you face difficulties in life, I urge you to not dwell on your suffering, but to give thanks for an opportunity to strengthen your faith. If you do these things, then you will gradually accumulate merit in your present life and will also build up a supply of merit in the spirit world. At the same time you will be making your guardian spirits happy, and they will reward you with better luck. This in turn will help make many other people happy. In effect you will have helped create a perfect pattern of circulating goodness. And in short, profit will have in this way come to equal merit. Furthermore, the fountain of good monetary fortune that the gods will offer to you will never run dry. You and your descendants will be able to enjoy its blessings for all eternity.

Talent Is the Key to Success

The man of genius often lives in his own little world and in many ways is oblivious to what goes on in the society around him. For that reason many such men have no luck in making their fortunes. But in cases where such a man has talent and is in touch with what is happening around him, then his talent can directly boost his good fortune with money.

Especially in this day when the quality most prized by contemporary society is harmony, people with AB blood type who have the ability to interact well with others have a better than average chance of getting ahead in life. This phenomenon is clear among the ranks of public officials, top managers and other leaders.

On the other hand, many extremely gifted people who stand out from the crowd find themselves shunned in many firms precisely because of their superiority.

So if you think you are the genius type, your best bet would probably be to get involved without hesitation in a venture business or go to work for a small or medium size firm that shows good growth potential. Or you might consider setting aside capital so that you can start your own company. There you could freely exhibit your personal talents to your heart's content.

There is an anecdote concerning the famous ninth century Buddhist ecclesiastic Kukai (774-835), whose posthumous title was Kobo Daishi, which I think makes an interesting distinction between the genius and the simply talented man.

As the story goes, one day Kukai received a letter, whose contents might be paraphrased as follows:

My superior simply will not take notice of what I try to tell him. If I remonstrate with him, he just gets angry and refuses to even lend me an ear. It has gotten to the point where it seems to me that the best thing to do might be to leave his service.

The author of this letter was a brilliant man; you might call him one of the genius types. But unfortunately his superior was just of mediocre ability. So even if he did recognize that the brilliant advice his subordinate was giving him was correct, because of his higher rank and his pride, it was not easy for him to act in accordance with the ideas of his genius advisor.

The gist of Kukai's reply to the troubled subordinate was this:

Correct advice exalts the righteous heart and from ancient times it has been extolled as good.

Nevertheless, the question is how to offer this counsel. Even should your logic and arguments triumph, that will not be enough to make people act as you would like them to. Therefore, the best thing to do is to explain things slowly until the other person comes around to your own way of thinking. The same holds true for handling your superior. If you act together according to his intentions and then point out how things have gone awry, then he will no doubt agree with your view.

Say, for example, you have two different plans – call them A and B. Despite the fact that you are convinced that B is the superior one, your superior refuses to have his confidence in A shaken. In such a case, do not waste your time debating in favor of B. Rather help your boss implement plan A.

Then when he sees that strategy fail, he will give up on plan A and accept your advice. That is the correct attitude to adopt.

In Buddhism this kind of attitude is known as *doji* or personal identification and empathy. When the Lord Buddha is guiding our actions, he similarly joins in performing the same action we are performing so as to lead us towards the good. Another phrase referring to the same phenomenon is *wako dojin*, an expression which refers to the willingness of Buddhas and bodhisattvas to disguise their true nature so as to mingle with human beings and help their souls achieve salvation.

Because the realm of the gods and spirits is so far superior to our own material world, even should the light of the gods and Buddhas be directed at us mere human beings, it would simply dazzle us and we would not have the faintest idea what it was.

Consequently, these superior beings themselves have to come down to this ephemeral world in order to save the mortals who dwell in it. And they have to adapt their message to the level of spiritual development of the person they are seeking to save. No matter how lofty the arguments they present might be, if the person cannot comprehend what they are trying to get across, then there is no way that he or she will accept them and the effort will have been in vain.

So the would-be savior does not reveal his full wisdom, radiance and talent to the person he is attempting to win over, but instead keeps these characteristics under the degree of control appropriate to the spiritual level that the person has attained. This is how the principle of *wako dojin* operates.

It might be considered as shorthand for the expression, "Softened (*wa*) is the light (*ko*) of the Buddha, when he shares the same (*do*) world of dust (*jin*) as men."

What is referred to here is the fact that since the radiance of the Dainichi Nyorai (*Mahavairocanasatathagata*), the supreme and universal "Great Sun" Buddha, is so overwhelming, he takes the form of a Jizo guardian deity, who gives off a soft, serene light and who prevails upon the various spirits of Hell to grant mercy to sinners.

So Kukai was suggesting that his correspondent adopt the same kind of attitude when he offered advice to his lord. And furthermore he advised that if that approach did not work, then the man should change his strategy. Kukai's letter was written in a placid, unhurried, very polite style that is difficult to do justice to in translation, or even in modern Japanese. Suffice it to say that the above quote merely paraphrases the contents of his actual letter.

As you can no doubt surmise from this letter, although a genius of enormous stature, Kukai transcended great difficulties and tribulations in his efforts to spread the doctrines of the Shingon (True Word) sect of esoteric or Tantric Buddhism, which he himself had brought back from China. Although he was only 31 when he became a Shingon teacher of the highest rank, we know from his memoirs that for over a decade he was (to his own mind at least) unsuccessful in spreading the doctrine. It would seem that far more than the man to whose letter he was replying, it was Kukai himself who was suffering from the failure of others to heed his advice.

In any event, the fashion in which this great genius Kukai went about building up a record of good deeds until he had finally accomplished what he had set out to do was very much in accordance with the spirit of *wako dojin*. Regrettably though, such instances in which the enormous talents that many people have inside of them are not allowed to find proper expression – because they are nipped in the bud by the difficulties caused by the necessity to deal with ignorant people – occur far too often. Talent exists in order to be brought to fruition. If we really think about the situation, it appears obvious that many of the geniuses in large organizations today are surviving by passing for mere men of talent. And things have probably always been that way.

Differences Between Kukai and Saicho

Saicho (767-822), whose posthumous title was Dengyo Daishi, was a contemporary of Kukai and along with him is considered one of the most important figures in the history of Japanese Buddhism. Instead of *wako dojin*, Saicho placed emphasis on the spirit of fastidiousness. His spirit and attitude were permeated by his belief that *what is right is right*. Believing that a certain path was correct, he also believed that men must follow this path completely. He therefore stressed rigorous training, austere living and strict monastic discipline. Here again we might call this teaching the thinking of a person of the genius type.

Why was it then that Kukai and Saicho, two men who had faith in the same Buddha, should come to think in such very different ways. I believe it can be traced to their very different personal histories.

Kukai endured great personal suffering in his life. And in addition that suffering was very much related to this present world. For example, on many an occasion he had to bow his head and nearly beg for permission to establish temples. As a saint who was willing to bow his head not only to the Buddha, but to common people as well, Kukai no doubt suffered great personal distress since he was by nature self-effacing and anything but power hungry. But these experiences helped shape his way of thinking.

Nevertheless, at times he must have felt shamed nearly unto death. No doubt he said to himself, "Why is it that I must bow my head to those who are clearly my inferiors in terms of intelligence, knowledge, spiritual strength and spiritual standing, especially since I have dedicated my entire being to the service of the Lord Buddha."

The history books tell us that Kukai was eventually able to win the favor of Emperor Saga despite fierce opposition from the religious establishment, cultivate his genius and leave behind an impressive record of achievements. But it is clear that since he lacked high birth and influential supporters in the highly aristocratic society of the times, where connections meant everything, he achieved his rank and renown almost entirely on his own.

Kukai preached that *desire more than anything is the central life force*. In other words, by sincerely confronting desire, we can for the first time learn what it really means to be a human being. The fact that he was able to achieve this insight is proof that Kukai was a true genius. I should note here that the personal attitude I think we need to adopt towards the gods should be based on Saicho's teachings, while we would do well to look to Kukai for hints on ways to deal with the world.

However, unfortunately in the spirit world Saicho holds a considerably higher position than does Kukai. Although Saicho struggled fiercely with the six Nara sects, the conservative establishment of the time, which took up much of his energy so that he could only accomplish half of what he wanted to do, his heart remained genuinely innocent. In addition, he had a fervent desire to educate the youth of Japan so that they would become the nation's greatest treasure.

On the other hand, Kukai was preoccupied with spreading the esoteric teachings of Shingon and as a result underwent considerable travail. Both were deeply compassionate holy men, but when it came to purity and breadth of feeling for others, Saicho was clearly the superior. Consequently, it was the eclectic Tendai school which he founded that became the mainstream of Japanese Buddhism, and it must be admitted that its teachings are more in align with the desires of the gods and the spirit world than are Kukai's.

Immediately after his death and entrance into the spirit world, Saicho was ranked seven positions higher than Kukai. And from the spirit world Saicho continued to do good. He attracted Honen, Shinran, Nichiren, Dogen, Eisai, Ippen Shonin and other later leaders to the spiritual center of Enryakuji on Mt. Hiei northeast of Kyoto which he had founded. He also gave them spiritual guidance from the other world.

In addition, Saicho worked hand in hand with Prince Shotoku, the greatest early fosteror of Buddhism in Japan, to offer new forms of the religion that would be appropriate to the circumstances in the country in each succeeding age and to help ensure peace and prosperity throughout the realm. For all of these achievements he was rewarded with promotion in the spirit world and ended up a full 24 ranks above Kukai.

In the meantime, Kukai's own spirit was being further purified and trained in the underworld, until finally in 1835, a millennium after his death and entrance into the spirit world, Kukai began a new round of spiritual activity. I explain all of this in greater detail in my book *The Divine World*. But, suffice it to say that during a turbulent period of transition in Japan a few decades prior to the Meiji Restoration he was reborn as Onisaburo Deguchi, the founder of the Omotokyo sect.

The lives of Deguchi and Kukai were filled with both successes and failures. But upon finishing his mission to lay the groundwork for a spiritual revolution (in the person of Deguchi) and his return to the spirit world, Kukai saw his rank raised many notches so that he ended up only two ranks behind Saicho.

During his lifetime of 78 years, Onisaburo accomplished things that only he was capable of doing. In the process, he underwent great trials and recorded enviable achievements.

In fact, during the 78 years that he was on earth in the subconscious of Deguchi, Kukai underwent so much personal testing and accomplished so much that he was able to acquire nearly the same amount of merit as Saicho did for his part in helping attract many generations of spiritual talent to Mt. Hiei and training them there over a period of more than a thousand years.

Unfortunately, while he was undergoing reeducation in the spirit world for more than 700 years Kukai was unable to provide spiritual assistance to the monks training on Mt. Koya, the mountain temple complex that he had founded. All he could do was moan about the lost opportunities. If only he had been less strong-willed and had been willing to simplify his teachings and make them more Japanese!

Still, Kukai's presence has remained in this world as a source of salvation for the common people and the role of Koyasan in Japanese religious history and civilization is beyond estimation. I have gotten involved here in a discussion of the relative rankings in the spirit world of Saicho and Kukai, but I would hasten to point out that I honestly have absolutely no desire to criticize either one of these two spiritual leaders. Furthermore, I am not in the position to offer such criticism.

Nevertheless, looking at things from the perspective of the Japanese spirit world, I would have to say that each of these men has been entrusted with a different kind of mission. This helps explain their relative importance at any given time in the material world and the spirit world. Both have been assigned a precious basic mission by ⊙ Su, the god of creation in the universe, who has overall control of the various dimensions.

Kukai's job is to play the father role and to help bring together human beings and the gods. Saicho on the other hand has the more maternal role of designing ways to cultivate human talent and show the proper path.

The greatest teachers throughout the history of Japanese Buddhism have studied at Mt. Hiei, finished up their training on Mt. Koya, and at the appropriate moment been inspired by the gods to preach a certain doctrine on their own. If Prince Shotoku might be said to have sown the seeds of Buddhism deep in Japanese soil, these two men, Kukai and Saicho, provided the *yin* and *yang* forces that they needed to grow.

For that reason, no one can really judge which one was superior or inferior. They were each needed, but for different reasons. The fact is that even though they might have initially been assigned different ranks in the spirit world, in the end they will both finish at the same level. In fact, they are both destined to reach the highest level of the spirits.

Gorgeous Flowers From Dirty Roots

As I already explained in my books *Lucky Fortune, Divine Help in Romance*, and *Divine Powers*, most people to a greater or lesser extent suffer from spiritual barriers. What I mean by the presence of *spiritual barriers* is that evil deeds of parents and ancestors have created bad karma for their descendants or these descendants themselves have engaged in evil actions which have unleashed spirits in search of revenge. They may even assume the form of the spirit of a large snake which causes illness or failure in business or other activities in the life of its enemy.

But the way in which these spiritual obstacles attributable to karma most directly manifest themselves is in how the individual thinks or looks at things. To put it simply, the man who is strongly

being influenced by karma tends to develop an extreme form of thinking and always feels he *must* do this or that. Similarly, once he makes up his mind, he is likely to lose all flexibility and sense of compromise. Such stubbornness, based on self-centeredness rather than principles or feelings of love, is a clear sign of karma at work.

In such cases, a person's thinking becomes dark and inflexible. When that happens, that person starts thinking of nothing but himself or herself and turns a deaf ear to the opinions of others. A person who becomes too fastidious is also as likely as not to fall into this deplorable pattern. If the beauty of the flower totally occupies the mind, then all thoughts of the humble root below the surface of the ground are banished from the consciousness.

That does not alter the fact that it is that root buried in the ground that supports the gorgeous flower. If you objectively compare the two, then without a doubt the root will lose out in any aesthetic comparison with the flower. But even so, it is ridiculous to ignore the life-sustaining role of the root. In order for a beautiful, healthy flower to grow, it must have a strong root beneath it to support and nurture it.

When it comes to human beings, you might think of desire and instinct as being the root. When Kukai pointed out the importance of desire for human beings, he clearly saw how its role was the equivalent of the root for the flower. As desire is essential for human beings, so too is the root for the existence of the flower. Kukai saw all this as a special form of *beauty*.

I have digressed a bit into a somewhat debatable area. But the point I am trying to make is that we human beings have sides to our nature that are not necessarily beautiful. By being aware of the root part of our nature that does not show on the surface, we can begin to comprehend what human beings are really all about.

44

Religious leaders and the charitable at heart sometimes prefer to look at only the beautiful and pure sides of humanity, and ignore the ugly sides. But that is a grave error.

The people who make it in this world, those who win the esteem of others, are invariably capable of clearly discerning both the flower and the root. If that were not true, then no one would look up to them and want to follow them. They can see the ugly side of things, but accept it. Such people are generous and broad-minded. They are destined to do well in life and to have great good fortune with money.

Righteous Power Versus the Forces of Evil

Why Are Only the Bad Good at Gambling?

In Japanese we have a saying that means: "Money ill gotten does not remain long."

Nevertheless, when you look at the way things are these days, you have to wonder whether scoundrels are not the only ones who can make their fortunes. In the past few years there have been several scandals in Japan in which silver-tongued devils have accumulated immense amounts of money through shady tactics. In some cases though, the schemes have backfired and ended in disaster and even death for the brash con artists involved. Thus karma decided that these individuals would reap a whirlwind.

But all of this really only represents the tip of the iceberg. True evil rarely shows its ugly visage for all to see.

It is sometimes said that anyone who uses dishonest means to make money will suffer in hell for his transgressions after he dies. Moreover, the punishment for his misdeeds will continue through the lives of his grandchildren.

Despite such words of warning, it often seems that the only people who attract money are crooks. It makes you want to cry at times. However, most people, myself included, continue to believe that the righteous will be rewarded with monetary success, while evildoers will get their just desserts, feeling that this is the true law of nature. That is the way the spiritual world thinks too.

But the situation seems to be quite the opposite in the real world, and the honest man often appears to be a fool. No wonder people ask themselves where the divine light could be shining, or otherwise want to grumble about the ways of the wicked world.

Could it be that the good man has a certain set of rules for making his money, while the wicked man operates by a completely different standard? Could that be the reason why all the big money seems to end up in the hands of the wicked?

At one time I was deeply disturbed by such doubts. But the point finally arrived when I clearly understood what is really happening. Why should the good man continue to lose and the bad man continue to win? Their respective lots in life can be attributed to differences in will power and perseverance.

I'll do whatever I have to to make money. If I have to shove the other guy out of the way or step all over him, that's all right with me. I'm gonna get rich no matter what.

Regrettably, this is the way the evil person thinks. But such a person's will to fight on is awesome. Whether asleep or awake, all he can think about is money, money, money. In extreme cases, he might even kill in order to cash in the victim's life insurance policy. His thinking becomes totally fixated on money and excludes everything else.

Such an obsessive way of thinking also prods the spirit world into action. Sometimes the thinking itself even transmutes into a spirit, what is referred to as an *ikiryo* or wraith, which literally takes possession of that person. In a certain sense you might say that thoughts and the spirit world are both in the same dimension. So naturally if a person thinks of nothing but money, money, money for an extended period of time, then the spirit world will be drawn near by the very force of the fixation, and good fortune regarding money will be the result for the person who is thinking these powerful thoughts.

But what about the so-called decent man?

Money? If we've got enough to let our family live decently that's enough. True if the kids get sick we don't have enough money to take them to the doctor's, which is worrisome. But we really don't need to live luxuriously. We'd never think of shoving the other guy aside to get rich. There are a lot more important things in life than getting rich.

It is obvious that in such cases the person is totally devoid of the thinking needed to make a fortune. If you lack desire and the right kind of thinking, naturally you are also going to lack the necessary tenacity. As a result, the spirits that provide good fortune are not aroused enough.

If you have a heads-on competition in money making between a decent fellow who has neglected to activate sufficiently the spirit world, and who lacks strong determination, the right way of thinking and tenacity versus an oily, unprincipled type who has his goals clearly identified, who has concentrated his thoughts in a way that has set the spirit world in motion to bring him good luck, and who has the awareness and tenacity to get what he wants, then it is quite obvious who is going to win in the end.

That is the reason why it always seems like the bad take the prizes.

Strong Desires of the Right Kind

Well then, does all this mean that the good people of the world are destined to always stand in the shadow of their more ruthless neighbors? Nothing of the sort. Generally the desires of good people are weak and those of the evil are strong. This difference in the strength of desires is reflected in a gap in spiritual power, will power or intensity. But if the decent person can strengthen his proper desires, he will have no reason to fear that he will be defeated by the power of evil.

There is really no need to seek solace in the belief that even though you may be defeated in the actual society of men, you will triumph over the wicked when you die and enter the world of the spirits, or otherwise engage in rationalizations. You can beat evil right here in this world. And you can triumph over it again after you die as well. This is the kind of just thinking that you should adopt.

I would like to emphasize that the degree of self-conviction and will power that you have translates directly quantitatively into the amount of good fortune that you can expect to enjoy.

If you have strong faith that *good will triumph over evil*, then your powers of concentration will increase naturally as will your stick-to-itness. Moreover, as your level of consciousness is raised, you will begin enjoying a situation in which your guardian spirits and other powers of the spiritual world will lend you their full backing. This is how you go about developing spiritual power for good fortune.

Most Japanese, from religious leaders on down to the common man, seem to be lacking in the thinking needed to make use of this proper form of desire. So because they lack this correct desire they find it impossible to vanquish powerful forces of evil. The man who spelled out in detail the way to affirm desire and turn it to good ends was none other than Kukai. And the list of those few men who in Japanese history adamantly refused to submit to spiritual, social or political evil, and who exquisitely showed the inherent power of the moral man includes Nichiren in the thirteenth century and more recently Onisaburo Deguchi, the founder of Omotokyo.

But one thing I must emphasize here is that even though I am advising that you wholeheartedly embrace desire, I must also warn you to avoid by all means building your world around yourself. Desire should never be equated with egocentrism.

Instead you should firmly believe that what the spirit world truly wants is not just your making money, but rather your playing a role to bring joy to the greatest number of people possible. With this principle in mind, you should dare to dream a great dream of goodness and then harness your desire to the mission of bringing it to fulfillment. Should, however, you not properly control this passion and become obsessed with money, money, money, then your spirit of perseverance will simply wither on the vine.

Come what may, we should retain strong faith in the philosophy of assigning at least 70 percent of what we do for the sake of others, for our company and for our customers. If you do that then you are justified in saying to yourself that the other 30 percent or whatever is likely to come your way. No, it is certain to come your way. We should pay heed in this regard to the thoughts of the late Toshio Doko, who in the last years of his life was the undisputed doyen of Japan's business world. Doko trusted in a "strong power that is working to bring about more good, to improve the situation and to bless people with greater happiness."

As I will explain below, if you pray to the Three Gods of Monetary Fortune and Seven Deities of Good Luck, you are certain to be blessed by good fortune beyond your wildest expectations.

Many people harbor the desire for good financial luck for their own benefit. But the number of people whose first consideration in desiring such good fortune is the will of the gods and spirits or the general happiness of humankind is truly very small. For that reason we need to find many more people who are willing to make use of the power afforded by the spiritual world.

And those who dare to have high hopes should be constantly on the alert that they do not let their dreams diminish to where they are only concerned with making money for themselves. They should bear in mind that if you set your goals high, the money might flow in small increments at first, but it will quickly add up.

Don't Touch Money Controlled by Devils

Let's consider exactly what this thing called money really is.

Why does money exist in this world? I am sure that quite a few of my readers must have asked themselves that question at one time or another. When we do not have a penny in our pockets, even before we start wishing we had some moola, we are likely to think, "The world would be better off if money and other riches didn't exist."

It is probably best to think of money as the ultimate thing on earth, the be all to end all in our materialistic world. The Chinese character used in Japanese for money can mean either a legal medium of exchange, such as yen or dollars, or the substance gold depending on how it is read. Gold of course has long served as a barometer of value, partly because no matter how many thousands upon thousands of years pass, it never rusts nor loses its shine. Even though as far as we know no one ever sat down and decreed that this should be so, the wisdom acquired by the human race over the ages naturally decided that this would be so.

Nevertheless, although in corporal form human beings belong to the material world, as far as the incorporeal spirit world sees things, human beings are a bundle of mind and spirit. But when this spirit (or individual soul if you will) is active, then it functions as four separate essences or faculties, namely the *kushimitama, nigimitama, sakimitama* and *aramitama*.

The *kushimitama* corresponds to the qualities of intellect and intuition. The *nigimitama* has the characteristics of friendliness and harmony. The *sakimitama* is an expression of the love and compassion in a person. And the *aramitama* shows his or her courage and fortitude.

So there is really one soul made up of four distinct spirits or natures. Furthermore, although the body eventually returns to dust, the human soul is immortal and non-material, enjoying a purely spiritual existence.

In other words, when a person is alive, he or she has one foot in the material world because of the body and one foot in the spiritual world because of the soul. But in essence the human being is really a spiritual being; the body is only borrowed. And the spiritual world is controlled by the forces of good, which I will refer to here as *kami* or "gods." (Actually, *kami* requires a rather complicated definition, which I will have to forego at this point.) On the other hand, the material world is controlled by evil spirits or "devils."

In addition, transcending and encompassing all good and evil is the Supreme Absolute which is almighty. Chinese philosophy refers to the forces of evil and good respectively as *yin* and *yang*, or evil spirits and benevolent deities. And the Great Void is the term used to refer to the universe before *yin* and *yang* were differentiated. If you think in these terms, then I think you will be able to grasp my explanation.

52

Incidentally, people who give themselves up entirely to desires of the flesh are in effect controlled by the forces of evil. But individuals who make the attempt to transcend the demands of the body and reach a higher spiritual plane are under the authority of the gods. I suspect that quite a few of my readers might be ready to dismiss this explanation as an example of "short-circuited thinking." But as one who can freely observe and listen to what is going on the realm of the spirits, I assure you that it is true.

I am not saying that the material world is all evil. But the devils want to see people possessed by the desire to control the material world or be totally preoccupied with that world. And there is evil in a heart that falls for their lures. Let there be no confusion on that point.

But now let us return to the question of money. When we become totally fixated on money, concentrate all our faculties on the pursuit of money, and fail to refine our souls and improve our inner being, then we have clearly fallen under the spell of the devilish kind of good monetary fortune.

Fall prey to the snares of these devils and you may be able to accumulate a lot of money, but you will also find that you will be incapable of functioning as a source of happiness for others and will be unable to lift your own soul towards the higher reaches of the spiritual world. Far from it. Your soul will become dissolute and hardened and despite the luxurious life you lead, you will be plagued by feelings of emptiness and anxiety.

But the devils are likely to plant thoughts like the following in your head: "What does it matter, just give me the money. All I want is to be able to enjoy the pleasures of the flesh to the fullest while I am alive, to drink the cup of excess dry. But for that you need money and lots of it. There's nothing more important in life than making money."

The point is that it is easy to fall for this kind of twisted thinking. Because of the nature of human desires, if we do not experience some kind of spiritual awakening, then we are likely to establish our standards for happiness based solely on the satisfaction of physical desires and thereby become captives of the devils.

Take the case of Christianity. Since the Kingdom of God is believed to be for those pure of heart, Christians yearn for the world of the spirit. Ironically though in their efforts to grow closer to God by providing more donations or building taller cathedrals and churches, many Christians have actually fallen into the snares of the Devil.

The real spiritual world is far more iridescent. There is nothing wrong with seeking our own satisfaction or fulfillment and we should never reject the pleasures of the material world. But we must esteem the proper balance between the spiritual and the material, and that means subordinating the latter to the former.

If when seeking good monetary fortune you always do so on the basis of the correct standard – namely the desire to please the spirit world, yourself and your fellow human beings – then you will attain the type of good fortune controlled by the gods. In other words, the varieties of good fortune provided – by the devils and the gods – are two totally different things.

Suspicious Odors

If we decide to adopt the credo *Let me be happy in this world, and I won't give a damn about what happens afterward*, accept the devils' "good fortune" and live a life of extravagance, what happens after we die and enter the spirit world? Well, I will tell you as a way to warn you.

Money is known in the spirit world as well as on earth. But it is only used in the lower levels of that world, and interestingly enough that money stinks. In fact it reeks like all hell. Even if you pinch your nostrils shut tight, the foul odor will still assault your organ of smell. The odor is unbearable, but since the denizens of these stinky precincts are forbidden to remove themselves to other levels of the spirit world, they just have to wince and bear it, even as the foul odor permeates their lungs and insides.

It is only people who relied on the good fortune of the devils to accumulate and spend their fortune who suffer this stinky torture from that ill-gotten money. In addition, because of the karmic laws this pile of money has been transformed into an enormous mountain of dung. And the children and grandchildren of the offender are doomed by their connection to this stinking mess in the spirit world to suffer while they are on earth.

On top of that, because of their inordinate greed while they were alive, the inhabitants of this particular corner of the spirit world all have pitch black faces that look like they have been completely painted with India ink. But since everyone else looks the same, nobody makes a big deal about it.

When discussing this home for those who relied on evil means for their good monetary fortune, I cannot help but be reminded of the famous Japanese folk story *Hanasaka jiisan* ("Flower-Blooming Granddad") about an old man who because of his good deeds was blessed by the gods. I will give an abbreviated version of it here.

One day an honest old man heard his pet dog barking in a field in back of his home. He went out to see what was the matter and found the dog standing on a certain spot yapping away. He began to dig there and before long a fortune in bright coins came jingling out.

When his neighbor, a greedy old fellow, heard about the incident, he tried to get the dog to do the same thing for him. But when the pooch showed no inclination to do so, he beat the animal until it finally stopped at a spot in the fields and started barking. When the nasty old boy dug there, he found an enormous jar. Overjoyed at the thought that he too had found his fortune, the nasty old man opened up the pot, but his glee soon turned to horror when a load of stinking shit shot out at him.

Another nursery tale that all small Japanese children learn *Shita-kiri Suzume* ("The Tongue-cut Sparrow") is very similar. This one involves an honest old man and the nasty hag who is his wife. But in this case, instead of shit coming out to give the evildoer her just desserts, snakes, lizards and horny toads do the service. But the plots of the stories and their morals are very similar.

Little children are taught through these folk tales that people should be honest and that if they are malicious, give in to all their desires, think only of themselves and do not give a damn about their neighbor, or engage in other forms of immoral behavior, then some day they are going to have to pay for their misdeeds like the nasty old man and woman in these stories did.

I have the hunch that spiritually acute men must have directly experienced the hell reserved for those who use their luck with money to evil ends, and that what they described became the basis of these folk tales which have been passed down through the ages.

Who Goes to Heaven?

The proverb *Money is the key that opens all doors* indicates just how powerful money is in the affairs of men. Is there any such standard against which everything is judged in the spirit world?

Let's forget the impressive mortuary tablets that are carved and posthumous names that are bestowed, the marble tombs that are built and the sutras that Buddhist priests are paid to read, all the things that are done to help out the dearly departed when he or she gets to the other world. Here I would like to describe what happens to people in the spirit world based on how they use their luck with money while they are still alive.

I already explained a little bit about the hell in the lower depths of the spirit world reserved for those who relied on the evil form of luck to make money while alive. How then should we conduct ourselves if we expect to enter Heaven?

First I should point out that Heaven is subdivided into three major levels. The highest is Number One Heaven, the next highest is Number Two Heaven and the lowest is Number Three Heaven. Of course everyone would like to enter the best neighborhood – Number One Heaven. But before you are assigned a rank you have to undergo a very strict qualifications investigation. If you do not possess the minimum qualifications, then you are not allowed to pass through the gates of Heaven.

It is much like the metal detector tests we must go through at airports; if even the slightest thing is wrong, then the buzzer goes off and you are not allowed to enter the country.

Those who clear this hurdle first enter Number Three Heaven. Most of its residents got here because regardless of what religion they belonged to, they led moral lives and used their own riches to help the poor or unfortunate. Of course, even if a person gives away mountains of money, if it was amassed through ill-gotten means to begin with, in other words if it was money made through the good graces of the devils, such philanthropy will be totally useless. The instant such a person arrives at the gate of Heaven the *detector* placed there to ferret out those with bad karmic connections will start wailing and everything will be revealed.

The next highest level is of course Number Two Heaven. Only those people who have lived blameless lives in which they followed the path of the gods and religion, and did as they should for themselves, their neighbors and the gods are allowed to enter into these hallowed precincts.

Then finally there is the highest level of the spirit world, Number One Heaven. This is a very special abode for the spirits of those people who while on earth followed the path of the gods to perfection, made a fortune in the proper way, earned rank and fame, used all their riches and position for the benefit of their fellow human beings and to please the gods, and as a result of all this left behind a long record of achievements.

These people relied not on the false fortune offered by the devils, but rather the strong power of good fortune provided by Heaven. And they made the most of the good fortune that came their way to give form to intangible virtue and were wholeheartedly backed up by the spirit world in their efforts. In other words, they were individuals who while alive sought to be one with the spirit world and to live a life of virtue, and thus were able to draw closer to the gods.

If we can tame the demands of the material world and the flesh so as to always conduct ourselves in accordance with the wishes of the gods, then we will be well on our way to Number One Heaven. But how successful have we been in overcoming the temptations of the good fortune offered by the devils and using the good luck bestowed by Heaven to bring joy to the gods and our fellow men? That is the key point that will decide whether or not when we return to the spiritual world we are allowed to enter Heaven.

How You Too Can Be a Success

There's a Reason Why You Haven't Made It

If there is no cause, there can be no effect. That seems pretty obvious. So if you cannot make it in the material world, in other words you cannot achieve the desired effect, there must be one or more causes for the situation.

The other fellow is a big success, but you are not even though you both joined the same company at the same time. What can be the reason for the discrepancy? Naturally there are many people who would very much like to know the answer to such perplexing questions. Let me tell you the real score.

As I already noted in the Prologue, if you want to see your hard work come to fruition, it is important to be ready when the moment of opportunity arrives, so that you can give full play to your talents. And in Chapter II, I will describe in detail how in this regard it is greatly to your advantage to enlist the aid of the Three Gods of Monetary Fortune (Sanmen Daikokuten, Zao Gongen and Sampo Kojin) and the Seven Divinities of Good Luck (Bishamonten – the god of treasure, Ebisu – the god of wealth and commerce, Daikokuten – the god of fortune and the five cereals, Benzaiten – the goddess of fortune, Jurojin – the god of longevity, Fukurokuju – the god of wealth and longevity, and Hotei Osho – another god of good fortune.)

Reliance on these deities is important in getting your chance for success and good material fortune, but it would be a big mistake to think that this is sufficient in itself. The reason is that success is not something that comes about entirely because of your own efforts. Remember the man who succeeds is given boosts by various people above him, has the support of friends and is backed up by his subordinates.

That is the real reason why he becomes a success. It goes without saying that for someone to become famous in this world and achieve a position of prominence, it is necessary for that man – no matter how talented he might be – to have his capabilities and true value recognized by others.

Everyone of us has our faults. But problems in interpersonal relations and communications can act as major impediments to our chances for success. It is imperative therefore for us to rely on the power of *nigi*, the spirit of harmony, to improve our relations with others. Incidentally, this *nigi* is the same *nigi* as in the adjective *niginigishii*, which means prosperous and merry.

The personalities of some of the famous military leaders of the age of disorder prior to Japan's reunion under the Tokugawa Shogunate might be regarded as exemplifying the four essences that collectively make up our soul. Oda Nobunaga, Tokugawa Ieyasu, Toyotomi Hideyoshi and Uesugi Kenshin represent the *kushimitama* (wisdom), *aramitama* (fortitude), *nigimitama* (harmony) and *sakimitama* (love) respectively.

And who among these four men accomplished the most? It was Hideyoshi, the poor peasant's son who united the empire. A perfect embodiment of the *nigimitama*. We should all bear this point in mind when seeking to refine our own characters.

My Experiences With Drinking

As is true I am sure for all of my readers, there have been times in my life when I have had serious problems, because even though I was aware of my character defects I found it impossible to correct them. Let me give an example from my past that might bring the problem into focus.

In addition to my spiritual activities as a psychic and researcher on the spirit world, I operate several companies. In other words, sometimes in my daily life I am acting as a spiritualist and sometimes as a business manager. I am operating these businesses while simultaneously engaging in spiritual activities because that is the will of the gods for me.

Now as any Japanese managers, businessman, or anyone who has done business in Japan extensively will agree, there is one unavoidable thing he has to do if he wants to succeed within the present structure of Japanese social culture and make greater profits for his company. I am referring to the need to socialize. Business deals in Japan are just not settled with a handshake after a cup of tea or coffee. And the more important the pending deal, the more time you have to spend socializing.

Even though I am a student of spiritual matters and believe myself to be treading a path approved by the gods, at times for business reasons I have to go drinking in the high-class entertainment district of Akasaka in Tokyo or similar night life areas. I like to refer to these districts as "*tanuki* cities." The *tanuki* (raccoon dog) in Japan is a symbol of craftiness and physical indulgence and the spirit dimension surrounding these "*tanuki* cities" is alive with the spirits of this wily animal, as well as floating spirits and drunken spirits. At first, I was not very fond of drinking, so I disliked going to such places.

Although I tried to hide my displeasure with having to be there, my expression and body language invariably gave away my true state of mind and it was not hard for the clients I was with to tell that I was not really enjoying their company. I kept telling myself that someone who cannot socialize properly will never be a success in the world of men. But even so, I found I could not change the way I felt.

Then one day I suddenly realized something important.

I thought to myself: "It's not always appropriate to be so pure and noble. If you're a real human being and a real spiritualist, then you should act more resolutely. The reason you can't drink and socialize properly is that your heart is too small, you're not the man you should be. Continue to act like this and your spiritual strength to overcome evil will wane. Just look. Your client is a man just like you. He undoubtedly has his good points, if you just look for them. Just relax and enjoy every moment of your drinking together. Just try and see how things work out."

"The trick in such touchy situations is to avoid evading what is bothering you and meet it head-on," I told myself. "Try to not adopt a negative attitude. Instead meet what comes to you with love and happiness. Believe that each encounter is not something which you have to endure, but instead an opportunity to learn. No, not just a chance to learn, something interesting in its own right. No, not just something of interest, something that can be thoroughly enjoyable. This is the way to go about things. If you proceed straight ahead like this, the way to go will naturally make itself known to you."

Once I had resolved to try a new approach, I started thinking to myself: "That's right. If you got all the millions of gods of Japan here together, the god of *sake* and the god of sociability would be in their ranks. From now on when I take that first sip, I'll consider it an offering to the spirit world."

From that instant I acquired the secret of drinking of the spirit world and from then on I have been able to keep up with the best of imbibers on the Ginza or in Akasaka. What has happened is that I have been blessed by the spirit world with a seemingly limitless capacity for tippling.

Now I can go all night without slowing down and match any of the big boozers I have met when out with clients on the town. In fact, I usually drink them under the table. Furthermore, although when drinking I can handle as many drinks as might come my way, at other times I do not feel the slightest need to touch a drop of alcohol. In other words, I have come to recognize that the gods have become my drinking partners. Although I guess I do not really have any reason to be especially proud of the fact.

Show You Are Human

I think there must be a lot of other people who have suffered as I have because of their inability to socialize. That is especially true for those who do not like alcohol or who do not care for the neon lights of downtown. What is easy and enjoyable for others can be a living hell for such unfortunates. But in Japan at least, if you want to be a success and want to make your fortune, learning to drink is something that is indispensable, so you should put a smile on your face as you seek to overcome the problem.

If no matter what you still cannot overcome your aversion to rubbing elbows over drinks, why not just try playing the fool once or twice. Of course when I advise you to play the fool, I am not telling you to really think and act like an idiot. Just think of it as a loosening up on purpose of the normal intellectual frame of mind we have on the job, a letting down of your hair, but certainly not any kind of sham.

It is often said in Japan that there are three keys to success: luck, frivolity and perseverance.

There is no need to explain what luck means. It boils down to being able to take advantage of the opportunities and chances that come your way.

Frivolity or foolishness refers to the desirability of not parading your intelligence before others, but rather seeking to mask it to a degree under the facade of appearing slightly foolish. Keeping the other fellow guessing, so to speak.

Perseverance is good old-fashion stick-to-itness, the willingness – and stubbornness – to hang in there until you finish what you set out to do.

Make no doubt about it, nowhere in the ranks of the captains of industry, the presidents and chairmen of major companies, or the men who are pioneers in their individual fields will you find anyone who is absolutely perfect from the top of his head to the tips of his toes. Every single one of these giants has something that might be called his Achilles heel. That is usually what gives them their charm or charisma. Consequently, socializing with such people is usually not awkward at all, and in fact the mood they create makes for some quite pleasant times.

You sometimes hear the expression *drunk on the mood*. So even if you do not care for alcohol, you might try to get high on the mood itself. In order to do that you must strip your heart of the ceremonial dress it is inclined to wear and learn to be foolish. The spoil sport could thus become the life of the party. And the party would become all the merrier as a result.

This attitude is effective even when you do not really care for the people you are with or find them difficult to get along with. The perfectionist is too often likely to reject others and crawl into his shell. That is hardly the way to become a success. Such a person usually proves to be a totally ineffective leader and cannot motivate

65

others through his sense of humanity. Needless to say, he is incapable of helping others either.

If you want to be a success in life and amass a great deal of money, then you will have to learn how to effectively handle in social situations even people who you do not like. That is because the more ability a person has, the more likely he is to have his own little quirks of personality.

It is fine if the other guy is willing to change his personality just for you, but in most cases you will have to make the effort to adapt to him. Besides, the experience of doing so will help to make your own personality more well-rounded. If you consider it all as a lesson in self-improvement then although it may be too much to ask that the face of a disagreeable client come to resemble that of the Buddha, his visage may at least take on a passing resemblance to your dear dad when he was snapping at you when you were small.

Strangely enough, if you act like this, before you even realize it your shell will fall away. And if you approach people in an open-minded manner, you will perhaps find to your surprise that the other guy will also start showing you another side of his personality. What we are really getting at here are the inner workings of human nature. This more than anything else is what I meant when earlier I touched on how to learn about the nigimitama spirit of harmony.

And when persons of real talent begin to say about you, "He's an easy guy to get along with," then you'll know good fortune is almost on your doorstep. When they begin declaring, "He's got promise," that means the needle on your "fortune voltage meter" is swinging upward. And when they say, "He can be trusted," you can be assured that good fortune and success are almost at the tips of your fingers. But if you really want to get them, remember not to prize yourself too highly. Instead, remember to reveal your own weak points sometimes, so as to show your generosity of character and your way of thinking.

Strong Faith and a Large Heart Attract Good Fortune

People who achieve great success usually have stronger faith, are more broad-minded and have a greater share of determination than do their neighbors. Of course, they are also more often than not well educated and highly skilled. Besides those people, tend to be blessed with good fortune and enjoy popular esteem. But what about those unfortunate people who do not have a better than average education or any outstanding talents. What can they do?

Success in education is really totally up to the individual. But when it comes to talent, luck and popularity, there are two types of factors involved – those predecided at birth and those resulting from self-effort in a case of Heaven helping those who help themselves. But even if you work as hard as you can, there are limits to the amount of talent and luck the gods will bestow on you.

So what you really need is a judicious mix of hard work, faith, confidence, resolution and a lot of soul. If you can put together that combination, the gods will not be at all stingy about sharing their spiritual power with you.

If you want to make it in the world and enjoy great material luck, you have to be prepared to accept the hills and valleys of the journey of life. A lot of things are going to happen during that marvelous trip. But just make up your mind that whatever you should meet – even typhoons or earthquakes – you will not let anything defeat you and that you will succeed and win your fortune.

Keep reassuring yourself that you are indeed being looked after by the gods and without any question are destined to be a lucky man. If you maintain such confidence and do not become faint-hearted, then the road to good fortune is certain to open up to you.

What happens is that your splendid resolve will set the spiritual world into motion to back up your efforts with spirit power. In other words, your forceful thinking takes the spirit world in tow. The man who makes it big in the world usually has many subordinates and can command large firms and big staffs. But just as important he can stir up the spirit world for his own benefit. So if you really would like to be a success, the most important thing you need to do is to become the kind of person who can enlist the aid of the spirit world and get it working for you.

Attempting to strengthen your determination is a process that of itself involves greater trials, but it can also win awesome backing from the spirit world. Every man and woman should want to see their spirit become as broad and free as the Pacific Ocean.

The Bald, Short and Fat Are Often Winners

Bald, short, fat. These have got to be the top three derogatory names flung indiscriminately at people. But surprisingly enough, if you are any of those three you have a better than average chance of being a success in life. Of course there are exceptions to this rule, but at least as far as the management ranks of Japan's top firms go, this seems to be the rule. But why should this be so?

Well, let's consider those who are small of stature first. If a person is short, he is likely to become pushy as a reaction to an inferiority complex and in turn become very strong of spirit. Furthermore, he probably got used to taking on those bigger than himself when he was a kid. So anytime he has the chance to compete with a really top-class opponent, his fighting spirit is more than likely to come to the fore and he is prepared to put out that extra effort.

So often times it becomes a case of: *the smaller the body, the bigger the heart*. And such individuals dream magnificent dreams. As a result, they can develop tremendous resolution. The famous warrior Minamoto Yoshitsune is said to be an example of this phenomenon.

Next, let's turn to the case of bald people. This condition is really physiological proof that the man concerned has more than the average quota of male hormones. It shows that the energy within his body is literally simmering below the surface till it bubbles over. This vitality is thus transformed into the power that helps the bald man make a success of himself.

From ancient times, there has been a saying in Japan, *There are no villains among the bald*. It's easy to regard the bald man as a good guy, partly because for some reason lack of hair seems to reassure. That is another plus for him.

So the bald man can enjoy a feeling of superiority towards those around him who have flowing locks. At the same time, by revealing what society considers his weak point, his physical defect, he helps to make his clients and associates feel more comfortable. The baldness thus works to the advantage of both sides. Thus, baldness makes for good business.

Last but not least, we come to the chubby club. It is a fact that in businesses involving service or direct contact with the public, roly poly people seem to do it better. In the United States and Europe the ideal image for presidents or supervisors seems to be not the rotund type, but the slightly thin, trim sort.

But that is because Western society places a premium on personal ability and the social structure itself is centered on individualism. And as a result executives do not have to worry about the kinds of complex interpersonal relations we have in Japan and in general do not have to think as much about how do deal with others as do their Japanese counterparts. I guess that if the emphasis is to be placed on individual capability, then the sharp, lean, tenacious type is best.

Although it is said that Japanese companies are also gradually being Westernized, corporate mores are still basically those of an agricultural people and human relationships cannot be considered solely in the context of work. Japanese coworkers are accustomed to going out drinking together and listening to each others gripes. And it is important to them to maintain family-like relationships. Japanese society of course takes note of individual talent, but especially appreciated are those people who are able to maintain smooth relations with others.

If we speak in terms of physique, it seems to be the chubby fellows who are most congenial. It is interesting to note in this regard that top executives at leading Japanese travel companies, that is people who have to be real pros in dealing with others, are most often of this type.

So, what I am saying is that if you are short, bald or chubby, that is hardly cause for despair. Rather, you should be able to gain self-confidence by telling yourself, "I'm executive material." As I explain in the following section on the Three Gods of Monetary Fortune and the Seven Divinities of Good Luck, such genial spirits are usually depicted as plump and beaming.

In fact I would go so far as to say people who faithfully conform to all three of these conditions but who are not successful and just cannot seem to get a hold of that old brass ring inevitably are being frustrated because of some extraneous factors.

Maybe you are fat because you are simply lazy and eat too much. Such conduct of course is out. Those are not the kind of people I am talking about. But if you have a manager who always retains his composure and seeks to calmly work out a solution no matter what kind of problem may arise, then he is likely to naturally tend to look like a laughing Buddha, or the gods Daikokuten and Hotei Osho.

Those who just sail through life with a favorable wind behind their back and have success and riches come flying to them as a matter of course really constitute only an infinitesimal portion of those who make it. Most people, I would say over 99.9%, progress down the path of success, amidst setbacks and losses, sadness and suffering.

Think Positive to Change Your Luck

But the fact remains that although two different people may face exactly the same difficult situation, one will simply bewail his fate while the other looks at it as a challenge and therefore something to be enjoyed.

Say for example there is a shipwreck and the survivors make it to a deserted island. The first type will say, "How could we have such dismal luck. First the ship went down, and now after drifting around we end up on this desolate, uninhabited island. Ah, we must be cursed. Now we have to suffer in this godforsaken place."

But the other type of person will say something like: "Great, we were saved from that shipwreck. What great luck. The gods are obviously with us. Well, until a rescue ship comes to pick us up, let's just take it easy here for a while."

The two men share the exact same objective lot, but which do you think is happier and closer to the gods. It goes without saying that it is the fellow who thinks, "What a lucky guy I am." The spiritual world likes this kind of thinking and so do other people. And people who think this way reinforce their luck, and cause people, money and even the gods to come rushing to their side.

I would like to cite the case of a young actress who came to me for advice to emphasize the importance of positive thinking.

Miss A, as I will call her, was at that time still a newcomer to show business, even though she had appeared on a few TV programs. Still great things were obviously expected of her. But almost as soon as shooting had begun on the film that she was making at that time, she had run into a big problem.

It was apparent how upset she was when she told me: "Sensei, the truth is I have to do a bed scene. And it's clear from the script that I'm supposed to play a woman who's known her share of men. But the thing is, this is just between the two of us, but I've only slept with a guy once and I don't think I could ever act like I was really making love. Still, there's no way I can get out of it, even though I'm embarrassed even thinking about doing such a bed scene."

The poor girl was squirming and obviously at her wits end. But it was also clear that if she could overcome this hurdle a successful and lucrative acting career awaited her. But it was just as clear that if she could not find a solution to her problem, then there was no telling whether her big chance would ever come again.

This is what I told her: "Among the most famous actresses around today, there are many who when they were young performed in the nude. But just because they stripped or appeared in a sex scene, doesn't mean that their spiritual state went to hell. The key was the spiritual strength of the performer. Whether such an experience turns a woman into a porno actress or whether she simply regards it as one step on her path to becoming a true actress

is all a matter of attitude. The question is how great is your resolution and how strong is your spirit?"

"Do you ever hear actors who play murderers whine that they've never really killed anybody. And what about artists who have to do a suicide scene. Of course not one of them has really committed suicide. But do you think they worry about how to get the exact look they would have as they reach the moment of death?"

"Isn't the ability to fake a bed scene when you haven't had the experience, the mark of a real actress? Adopt the attitude that since you are a real actress it is only natural that you should be able to pull it off right. Have confidence in your own acting, accept any challenge that comes along and take advantage of any chance that might come your way."

After listening to my advice, the face of the young actress brightened up and she said, "I see." And she promised to try her best.

To advance or retreat. When you are standing at that important crossroads and all kinds of problems are staring you in the face, that is really when you have the best chance to make success and good fortune your own. Because if you have the frame of mind that will look for the positive in every situation and the requisite power of spirit, then you will know for sure at that juncture which path you should choose.

The successful man is he who when he arrived at the forks in life's road was ready and willing to take advantage of his chances.

Methods of Moneymaking Differ With Age

Better to Be Poor When You're Young

A man of charm doesn't need money or power. The type of man described in this old saying is really a dandy or stud who can have his pick of women. That means he is most likely a young man. The real meaning of this saying is somewhat different, but for our purposes this explanation will do. And in this case we should interpret *money* as good fortune with money or actual wealth. And power really means influence.

So if we accept these definitions, then this saying can be reinterpreted as meaning, "When you're young, you don't have any influence or expertise and can't save any money." Well, that discovery is certainly not earthshaking news for anyone.

As apparent as that may be, this statement still contains a great deal of fundamental truth. From ancient times, the Japanese have been fond of saying, *Hardships forge the character of the young.* You might also say that it is bad for a person's mental health to be preoccupied with making money from when he or she is young. Of course when we are young we have to worry about making a buck, but we also should be concerned about improving ourselves as individuals and developing strong human qualities.

It is truly sad to see someone who has thoroughly enjoyed his youth, but who becomes progressively more wretched as the years go by. It is better to strengthen yourself through hardships. That way, today becomes better than yesterday and tomorrow will be better than today. This I believe is the correct approach to adopt.

If you are poor, then you come to appreciate the true value of money. Precisely because you do not have money, you also learn the virtue of perseverance. And lacking the wherewithal, you learn to find ways that do not cost money to enjoy yourself. Because the pockets are empty, you start to think about the real meaning of life.

For young people, a lack of money can actually prove to be the stimulus that makes them grow up into strong adults. Also, young people still are blessed with flexibility, and they are literally brimming over with potentiality. And the cares that come from want of money can be done away with through activity.

Resolve at 18 Means Reaching Your Peak From 30

So if it is only natural that the young should be poor, from what age can they expect to start entering the zone of monetary fortune?

The circumstances for women are rather special since for most of them marriage represents a world of entirely new dimensions, so what I am writing about now will not exactly fit their circumstances. (Actually, I go into some detail about the question of marriage and how women can help their husbands to be successful in my book *Divine Help in Romance*).

But men need to learn resolve when they are 18 or 19. In other words, I am referring to the period after they have reached puberty when they are just on the threshold of adulthood. At this time the attention of their consciousness is shifting from their inner self to society and their country. And for the first time they begin to think in some depth about their capabilities and talents. This is also the time when many men change guardian spirits.

Once you show the necessary resolution and win the backing of your guardian spirits, then the next thing to do is to acquire and consolidate the basic educational skills, sense of humanity and other attributes you will need for the rest of your life. This should be done by the time you are 25. While you are busy doing so, you also need to decide in which field you can best display your talents. However, until then you should do everything possible to develop your inner world and to add to your capabilities.

When you reach 30, it is time to let all the creative power that has been building up within you explode. Often somewhere between age 30 and 33 a person reaches the mental level equivalent to that which he attained in his previous life. In other words, if in his last life he had lived to age 80, he will now be able to draw on all the knowledge and capabilities he had acquired during those four score years, since they are stored in his subconscious.

But let me hasten to warn that this does no hold true for just anybody. It works only for the person who has been working as hard as he can up to that point and who has been living in accordance with the wishes of Heaven.

But these lucky people really are able to draw on the skills and capabilities that they won through hard effort in their previous lifetime when they are still only 30, which gives them a big advantage over their rivals. In fact, from about when you reach 30, your spirit starts *orienting itself outwards*. But when I say orienting itself outwards, I do not mean that your soul actually separates itself from your body. Rather your personal strength, in other words your spiritual force, brims up and out from your inner world and begins to project itself outwards.

But likewise it goes without saying that those men who reach 30 without having adequately developed their personal resources or having raised their inner world to the appropriate level begin to feel a great deal of consternation about what lies ahead of them.

Probably some among my readers who will soon be 40 are thinking, "It's already too late!" Well, I have got some special advice for people who consider themselves in this category about how to gain *super will power*. I am confident that it will help you to tap the full potentiality of your soul, make full use of your inner world and *spirit power*, and thereby express all your capabilities. Incidentally, the points I make in this regard can just as easily be made use of by men under 30, especially young businessmen who have just entered their company.

For the first three months, I want you to work flat out like a madman; work so hard that you think you are going to drop dead. Totally forget about your usual moaning and groaning. Do your very best at work, of course, but even when you are going to the toilet, riding the trains or zipping up in an elevator, attempt to concentrate totally on what you are doing.

Get so totally involved in what you are doing at any given instant that you forget you even exist. Just keep going until you finish what you are doing. This total concentration can be directed towards your work or towards the development of your personal abilities.

The next phase lasts for three years. During these next three years, I want you to get your life in order. Here you should strive to regulate carefully your clothing, food and housing so that everything is in tiptop shape. Try to win the prize in your work section for never being absent or tardy, or leaving early. And of course do your job to the best of your ability: prepare thoroughly ahead of time and be willing to put in overtime when necessary. "Yeah, yeah, I know all that. If only it were possible," you are probably saying to yourself.

But let me reassure you, if you have done everything you were supposed to during the first three months, and blocked out all the outside *noise* like I suggested, then your inner person and the lineup of the spirits who are supporting you will probably have undergone many dramatic changes. For example, there is a strong possibility that you will now have some different guardian spirits. Or at the very least, since your will power has increased tremendously, so too will the number of protective spirits who are prepared to back you up.

I do not have the slightest doubt on that score. And as strange as it may seem, what used to seem so difficult, now seems as easy as pie. You will also find your luck picking up very quickly and you will be able to handle just about everything very well. By this time, you will have more than your share of courage, energy and stamina. So after three years, you will find that an almost brand-new you has appeared on the scene who is super dynamic.

After this happens, you are in the position to build the best possible personal base and naturally display your full capabilities and talents. That is because now your personal spirit will have become firmly defined and your guardian spirits will be in the position to back you up fully. It is very important to you to realize what is really happening here.

Try Three Times as Hard

What I mean to say is that after we reach age 35 every one of us begins to lose some of our physical strength quite quickly. As our stamina wanes, so too does our will power. Furthermore, since most men by this time have a wife and children, they cannot be as adventurous as they were when they were young bachelors. Consequently, it is important for us to have experienced as many different types of things as possible by the time we reach 35.

After 35 we enter a period when we should try various things based on the competency we have acquired up to that point. Then when we get into our 40s, our physical strength decreases by the day and we also notice how our brain tires and we are becoming very forgetful.

The bell of the Gion Temple echoes the impermanence of all things.... This famous passage begins the classic *Tale of Heike*. It perfectly sums up the futility of trying to turn the clock back. All the ranting and raving we want to do will not retard our physical deterioration one bit.

Be that as it may, men who have throughout their thirties steadily improved their individual skills often find that their forties can be the best years of their lives, since they are mature and can separate the essential from the superfluous. So since their physical strength is petering out, they learn to rely on their management skills. Their fifties then become the period during which they can fully realize these management capabilities and help train their successors.

But that is not to say that there are no methods for mitigating the loss of physical strength during our forties – the so-called *hell of physical decline*. The key is to always remain *hungry* inside and to resolve to put out three times as much as the next guy. That means doing more than the norm to tap steadily your reserves of tolerance, ability to get the most out of what you read, and perseverance. If you manage to do that, then there is no reason why younger men should be able to out-compete you.

Still, you may ask how you can manage to remain *hungry* after you have reached middle age and continue to hang in there at such a flat-out pace. Earlier, I argued that we should not reach our full capabilities when we are still too young. The same rationale also applies in this context. The young man who reaches his full potential has no room left to grow. But if you still have that margin to grow when you have reached your forties and fifties, then you

will be in the somewhat abnormal position of constantly being hungry. But it is important to self-discipline the spirit, so as to create this feeling of perpetual hunger.

The best thing to do is always to try to remain slightly horny, while consciously remaining from expelling your semen. That is because controlling the libido helps build up your mental power, vigor, life force and concentration, and because this in turn becomes the basis of new spiritual power. But those who are willing to make a wholehearted effort to attain the goal will always feel mentally young. And you can still continue this process of growth even then.

Men who achieve this state of remaining constantly hungry even in their middle age should consider trying something totally new. For example, there was Ino Tadataka (1745-1818), who retired when he was 41, and then went on at age 51 to become an astronomer. Eventually, he drew the most precise map of Japan available at that time. There are several such cases of individuals who only entered a field in their forties or fifties but who ended up making contributions that got their names in the history books.

Get Ready for the Afterlife

Let us say you have worked hard all your life and at last you are about to reach retirement. Well that also is the time when you should start making preparations to enter the spirit world. Now I know some of you are going to say, "There's no such thing as an eternal life, so please don't remind me of my mortality."

But the fact is that when every man or woman reaches age 61 – a very important birthday by Oriental means of reckoning since it signifies the completion of a full life cycle – it is time for him or her to start thinking earnestly about the spirit world.

If you ask why I say that should be so, let me point out that by the time a person reaches age 61, his or her rank in the spirit world has more or less been determined.

The *kanreki* or 61st birthday represents the completion of one cycle of the ten calendar signs and twelve zodiacal signs. So everything begins again from this point. And there is a reason sixty full years should mark the completion of one cycle. It is at this point that the spirit world examines the individual to determine whether or not he did the things he was supposed to have done while here on earth. It is something like a graduation paper at college, a prerequisite for graduation. That is why one cycle finishes then.

The spirits hold a rigorous examination of a person's entire life up till that point. All the good deeds done by a person during the previous sixty years count as pluses, while all evil deeds that caused unhappiness for others count as minuses. After the tallying is completed, the individual is assigned a rank in the next world. However, since the spiritual world is compassionate, should a person use the remainder of his or her life for doing good, and thus merit a higher rank, then naturally the kanreki decision can be modified.

So people who have built up a fortune of ill-gotten gains would be well advised to return the money at once to its rightful owners. In addition, if it seems likely that your estate is going to cause domestic trouble among your heirs, then just keep enough for your wife and yourself to survive on and give the rest away to charity, after setting aside appropriate amounts for each of your heirs. People who unwisely leave behind gargantuan estates when they enter the spirit world, thereafter often find themselves preoccupied with what is happening to it rather than concentrating on their spiritual training.

Travel Can Be Fulfilling

Some of you are probably thinking that you will not leave any inheritance worth worrying about behind, but since you have already passed your sixty-first birthday, you would like to find some easy, tactful way for raising your future rank in the spirit world.

But to be frank, you will not be able to advance your rank through any such special method. The key factors are the state of your own soul, the merit you have acquired by bringing happiness to other people, and the degree of self-awareness you have achieved in the deepest recesses of your consciousness. In any event, if your own heart has not opened up and reached its full potential, then nothing productive can be achieved. And one way to cause this blossoming of your entire being is to travel.

Traveling with your spouse or lover is highly recommended. Together you can leisurely enjoy scenic spots or hot spring resorts. When choosing your destination, opt for the most enchanting scenery and the hotels or inns with the very best cuisine. If you can release everything that is pent up inside of you, then that would likely orient you in a lucky direction. But it is not really necessary to worry too much about all that.

But do be sure that you thoroughly take in the gorgeous scenery, savor the full taste of the exquisite food and let the waters of the hot springs warm the very core of your being. Refresh both mind and body to the extent that you feel like a brand-new man or woman. Attaining this special glow is what we are really looking for. After making the rounds of the hot spring resorts in Japan, it is time to start exploring the possibilities for foreign travel. Visit regions you had till now only dreamed about, experiment with unfamiliar cuisines and be startled by strange experiences. Such activities will restore vitality to your spirit.

Most people tend to get caught up in the tedious routine of everyday life as they get on in years. And less and less often does excitement enter their lives. Consequently, they lose their freshness. If a flow of water is dammed and it collects as a pool at one spot, it will grow stagnant and putrid.

The same holds true for people. If we live lives which are totally devoid of change, then our inner beings atrophy. For that reason as well, after you pass the all-important kanreki turning point, force yourself to get out on the road and travel. Notice how many older Western couples enjoy foreign travel.

Anyhow, let me give you an example of what I have been talking about from among the cases of people who visit me for advice. The example I would like to cite is that of a fine 70-year-old woman in Chiba Prefecture near Tokyo who operates a *sake* brewery. Actually, she is more or less retired. But when she came to me she was very worried about one thing, namely her 50-year-old son who has not been having much luck with the *sake* business.

The old woman was obsessed with worry about the family *sake* brewing business. The brews of the last three years had been disastrous. And she asked me, "What about the sake to be produced this year? What about my boy?"

Now I could understand her worrying to an extent about these things, but enough is enough. After all, her boy was already fifty years old and the president of the company. Was she really at an age when she should be worrying about such things, I ask you?

So I looked at the situation through spiritual eyes and was able to discern this old woman's figure in the spiritual world. She was in the section of the spiritual world where the inhabitants are constantly fretting about others – really it is a part of Hell. But at the same time, I should emphasize that it is the part of Hell where souls suffer the least. Its inmates have to stay there for three hundred years. When I ventured to tell the woman where she would be going to if she were suddenly to pass away, needless to say she seemed a bit shocked.

"Is that so? Oh my goodness," she blurted out.

"Stop worrying about the *sake*-brewing," I admonished her. "Leave it all up to your son. And as for yourself, what you need to do to raise the future rank of your soul in the spirit world and realize your true potential in life is to spend some more of your money. Look, you're already seventy, so start treating yourself the way you should."

In such a case, instead of going to the Hell for Worriers, it is far better for such elderly people to take the appropriate steps to dispose of their inheritance and arrange the payment of the relevant taxes ahead of time and then get out on their own, spend a little of their hard-earned money and enjoy themselves. Travel to the idyllic hot spring resorts scattered around Japan is an ideal way to accomplish this. Besides, if a dutiful son sees that his aged mother is bright, cheerful and enjoying herself, that undoubtedly will ease his mind.

Incidentally, the highest level of Hell that I have been referring to is very similar to our own world just after dusk, when everything is bathed in half-light. It is certainly not bright. Its drab tones are a perfect reflection of the hearts of its inhabitants. It is not the kind of place where you would like to make an extended stay.

The way we experience things in our real world is also the way we will experience them in the spirit world. If you view this life as being something beautiful, then you will be able to continue to see it as such when you get to the spirit world. And you will be able to relive vividly the tastes of all the scrumptious foods you ate when you were alive. It would also be good to bear in mind that the intangible merit you leave behind and the way you perceive things will determine the part of the spirit world you will go to after you die.

CHAPTER 2
Righteous Spirit Power Makes for Good Luck With Money

The Gods of Monetary Fortune

The Principle of Shinsoehikae

Everything has its fundamental cause. If you want to see your honest efforts rewarded by the gift from the divine world of the power to have good luck with money, then you must be cognizant of the various processes by which this good luck is bestowed by the gods. Let me stress the importance of this point.

The same principle operates in our human society. For example, should you return home and find a present of delicious fruit sitting on your desk, you will naturally ask your family members, "What's this all about?" If they answer, "Mr. A brought it because of the favor you did for him," then you're likely to say, "Oh, is that right?" And the image of Mr. A's face is likely to be in your mind as you enjoy the gift.

The same situation holds true when it comes to good luck. If you just keep begging to the gods, "Please, please," then even should you be blessed with good luck, you will likely just snap it up and make use of it without being truly appreciative of the great honor. Consequently, you will not be able to offer heartfelt thanks. As a result, the divine world will be cold to any repeat requests from you for assistance. That is the most important point to bear in mind when it comes to handling good luck with money.

Shinsoehikae or "complementary balance" is the key pattern here. This phrase *shinsoehikae* is actually taken from the art of *kado* or flower arrangement and refers to a situation in which the flowers are restrained backwards, so as to achieve the proper balance between the main part and subsidiary parts. Such an arrangement can achieve remarkable harmony. This basic principle used in flower arranging to attain the desired aesthetic effect is a perfect symbol of how the divine mechanism for drawing good luck to your person works.

The first thing to bear in mind is the importance of *shin*. Everything starts with Ama-terasu-o-mi-kami, the Sun Goddess. All blessings originate in her person. There are other major deities, including Ame-no-mi-naka-nushi-no-okami ("Master-of-the-August-Center-of-Heaven"), Hokuto-no-Kami – God of the Big Dipper, Kuni-toko-dachi-no-mikoto ("Earthly-Eternally-Standing-Deity"), Princess Kikuri, Dainichi Nyorai and Yahweh. They all exist, it is true. But at least for Japan, the Sun Goddess is the one who actually bestows the blessings. She is in effect the "Chief Director" or first among equals in its divine world.

Among the "Directors" beneath her we should include her brother Susa-no-o-no-mikoto ("His-Swift-Impetuous-Male-Augustness") and O-kuni-nushi-no-mikoto, as well as lesser gods such as those worshipped at the shrines of Usa Hachiman, Kajima, Katori and Sumiyoshi. According to their various functions and personal characteristics, they can be regarded as directors responsible for operations or sales. And of course they have all been entrusted with the power to make decisions in their own right.

The deities who are in closest contact with human beings are the local tutelary gods. And the creation gods Izanagi and Izanami, who gave birth to the Japanese islands, might be regarded as the founders of the firm, the Co-Chairpersons of the Board. Having retired, they have passed on the power to represent the firm to their beloved offspring.

This power of representation is none other than the central divine power that derives from ⊙ Su, the absolute god of cosmic creation and the diverse dimensions.

The Sun Goddess as President of Japan, Inc.

When the divine world established the equivalent of a foreign-capital conglomerate, it gave the divine authority in this sector to Jehovah, or Yahweh, the god of the Hebrews. He became the god of the Europeans. But we Japanese are not "employees" of a creative production company run by Ame-no-minaka-nushino-okami or the Kuni-no-toko-tachi Construction Firm. Much less are we on the staff of the headquarters of a foreign-owned stop-and-shop store or an Inari shrine. As long as we remain in Japan, we are full-fledged, lifetime employees of a Japan Incorporated that represents and embodies every last one of the gods of the land.

For that reason, we – the members of Japan Inc. – need to look to our Chief Managing Director, the Sun Goddess Ama-terasu-o-mikami, as the center around which all our efforts revolve. Compared to the other deities, the Sun Goddess is endowed to a greater extent with the virtues of moderation, harmonious perfection and self-fulfillment. She is the deity who bestows on us the benefits of *will power, brightness* and *ever expanding creative development.* She is also the President of the Japanese people. For that reason, it is only natural that the corporate nature of Japan Inc. (in other words, the national characteristics of Japan) should be bright, highly creative and action-oriented.

At first glance the essence of Japanese culture might thus appear to be very *feminine*. But as is suggested by the story in the *Kojiki* which relates how five male deities suddenly appeared from a divine necklace known as the Ihotsumisumaru, the *Yamato damashii* or spirit of Japan is also imbued with resoluteness and courage.

In the profoundly subtle operations of the divine world, another god may be the primary god for another people when it comes to good luck in money matters and prosperity in the material world, but for the Japanese people Ama-terasu-o-mikami always plays that role. So if you do not give the Sun Goddess her proper due, then you can hardly expect to see this good fortune come your way.

It is true that by relying on dragons, *tengu* goblins, Inari foxes, and white snakes you might get rich. But when you consider the big picture and take into account the harm that might result from an incorrect approach and how you in the afterlife and your descendants might suffer as a result, it is clear that the only kind of good fortune you can really afford to count on is righteous fortune that is correctly bestowed by the divine world.

Well, it seems I have gotten off on a bit of a tangent. So let's return to the main argument. But I just want you to bear in mind why you need to make the Sun Goddess the focus of your thinking.

The next principle we need to worry about is *soe*. If Ama-terasu-o-mikami is the main concern, the tutelary gods can be considered of secondary importance. These are the local gods that belong to one particular place on earth. They control the local spiritual world. As I explain in detail in my books *Lucky Fortune* and *Divine Help in Romance,* these gods watch over you from the day you are born until you get married, helping you to make the right choices in life. Since the activities of these gods are firmly rooted in the place where you live, they can help you greatly in your daily life and their actions (or lack of action) have a great bearing on whether or not you will become wealthy.

To go back to our analogy of Japan as a business enterprise, the Sun Goddess is the President who issues the orders to the tutelary gods. They in turn pass them on to the people living in their immediate neighborhood. Furthermore, the type of good luck with money that these tutelary gods provide is comprehensive. You will be able to develop your business, preserve your pool of talented manpower, increase your circle of good customers, come up with new products, and so on. Whether we are talking about the individual or a corporation, if you follow the lead of your tutelary gods in every respect, then you will turn into a winner in every respect. Every move you make will bring more money and success. This is what we mean by true, legitimate good luck with money.

Incidentally, there are some people who think that instead of seeking the assistance of Ama-terasu-o-mikami by a pilgrimage to her grand shrine at Ise, a far quicker and surer way to get wealthy is to worship at an Inari fox shrine. They probably base this assumption on their personal experience. But they should know that if they really believe that, then their experience is insufficient.

It is true that the foxes at these shrines might deliver good fortune to you, but the price exacted for the favor is often very great. For a detailed explanation of this matter, kindly consult my book *Divine Powers*.

Immediate Help From the Tutelary Gods

The divine blessings bestowed by Ama-terasu-o-mikami at Ise represent the same kind of never-failing good fortune as that which allowed Konosuke Matsushita, who was known as *the God of Management*, to accumulate an incredible fortune when he was alive through the sales of electrical and electronic merchandise. The blessings given by the tutelary gods are akin to the good fortune of a company which is able without undo strain to increase its sales and improve other business results, while maintaining annual growth of at least ten percent.

Furthermore, the typical pattern is that the Ise variety of luck usually takes at the earliest three to six months, or at the latest three years, to come your way. As a general rule, the more important the deity, the more time it takes to receive the divine favor. That is why you have to expect some time to pass before the benefits materialize.

On the other hand, the beneficence of the tutelary deities – the divine allies with whom we are in the closest contact in our daily lives – can in the fastest cases help you out the very day that you make your request. But even in the longest of cases, it will without fail assist you within half a year. Naturally, if you continue to entreat the local gods and pay visits to their shrines without your zeal flagging, then you can expect to receive the full benefit of the gods' favor faster and it will be more potent.

So as you can see, the more important the god, the longer it takes to receive his blessings. And conversely, the less important the deity, the quicker he can be expected to deliver. It is because of simple ignorance of this fundamental law of the divine world that some people think that it is most effective to pray at Inari shrines. My apologies, since it seems that I am digressing once again. Let us get back to the main point. But I do want you to bear in mind the above mentioned difference between the central aspect and the secondary aspects and their interrelation.

The final principle to consider is *hikae*. So, as you can see, it is through the gods that good fortune comes our way. The Three Gods of Monetary Fortune, who I will discuss in more detail later, take action at the request of Ama-terasu-o-mikami or respond on their own to those portions of a person's prayers that have not been taken care of by the tutelary deities. Once they know what a worshipper wants, then they can *power up* his or her chances of attaining those goals.

These particular gods occupy the dimension of the divine world closest to the material world in which we human beings live our lives. They occupy areas near the material world that are on the same spiritual level as the Buddha world known as *gongen* or "Power Reality" (so named because there the powers of avatars are temporarily manifested).

These are very welcome deities whose special function is to fill the gap when the *shinsoe* mechanism proves inadequate, for example when it looks like you will not be able to raise the capital you need by the end of the month.

These gods are really there to come to the rescue when needed. So it can hardly be said that the type of good fortune they bring is orthodox. Put another way, if the *shin* and *soe* can be looked upon as the "offensive" or "dynamic" form of good fortune, then this *hikae* is the equivalent of the "defensive" or passive form. The dynamic form remains the most important; the passive, defensive form is supplementary. That is the basic nature of their relationship.

Let me tell you a story instructive in this context. When I first started my companies, nearly every single month I was hurting from cash flow problems. I still remember clearly how on one occasion it was only three days before the close of the monthly accounts and we were still short by ¥5 million. I fretted over what we could do. Despite trying all kinds of things to raise money, prospects did not look at all bright. I thought to myself, "Why is it that although we are following the way of the gods and trying to operate this business properly and giving our everything on the job, we always seem to be strapped for funds. Are there really gods and Buddhas watching over us?"

So I prayed, "If you are really there, then please send some money before the three days left in the month are up. My prayers are not in the least motivated by selfish desire. I feel it my responsibility to allow our employees to develop fully their individual talents and I have a strong sense of trust in and duty to our customers. It is indeed a form of love. That is the truth. Please answer my prayers."

So I prayed for all I was worth: to the millions of gods of Japan and the almighty ⊙ Su. However...Well, I can say it now, never did I feel so disappointed in the creator of the universe, the god ⊙ Su, than in those dark days. I thought to myself that no matter what grand plan he might have or how benevolent he might be, I could not escape from the fact that if I did not get my hands on ¥5 million within the next three days, then all our magnificent plans would be for naught. Everything would be utterly and completely finished.

It was then that I realized that it was not always a case of the higher the dimension in which a deity existed, the better. Rather every deity had a certain role to play. And it finally dawned upon me that ⊙ Su could not do everything by himself. Even though ⊙ Su might be all-knowing, he has entrusted the execution of certain tasks to individual subordinate deities. That is the way things are actually handled in the divine world.

This situation is much like cases in the business world in which an outstanding manager will take full advantage of the combined capabilities of his subordinates and subtly seek to give them opportunities to display their strengths to the fullest. This is in accordance with the belief that the boss who insists upon invading the turf of his subordinates is not deserving of respect.

Three Powerful Allies

Well anyhow, back to the story. As you remember, I was beside myself because of my cash flow problems. I finally figured that if ⊙ Su would not help me, then I would just have to search for a deity who would. So while continuing to pray with all my heart, I searched for a god of the righteous world of the divine who would be sure to provide me with the ¥5 million before the three days were up. And in the end I found him: Sampo Kojin, the Kitchen God.

In fact, what happened was that the Sun Goddess ordered me in an august voice: *Worship Sampo Kojin.*

That was the first time I made the acquaintance of this venerable deity, who is the "strongest medicine" available when you have to raise money quickly at the end of the month. The Sun Goddess and Sampo Kojin personally gave me a quick course on the proper way to worship him; a procedure that is known to few, I might add. I performed this worship exactly as told to and the very next day I received ¥5.3 million. It was nothing less than a miracle. It was just as the sage Confucius had said: *Heaven is just and merciful.*

At that time I was up to my neck in debts: to the banks, to my friends and relatives, to the families of my associates in my spiritual enterprises. So I made my appeal to the gods when every other exit was blocked. Just at that point, I got a call from a customer who apologized for always paying me late and promised to settle his account the next day.

But it would not be completely truthful to say that the money just dropped down from Heaven. An employee at one of my companies, knowing what a bind we were in, had contacted the client and asked him to make payment as soon as possible. So I guess you can say that Sampo Kojin had sent the ¥5.3 million in response to the actions of men. That is the way Sampo Kojin, the ultimate protective deity, works.

Thereafter, through my careful investigations in various spiritual dimensions and Buddha worlds I came to realize that Zao Gongen is the deity responsible for business sales and Sanmen Daikokuten plays the same function in regards to marketing expansion. So I installed images of these gods in my personal "god shelf" after the Sun Goddess granted permission and instructed me in the proper rituals for their worship.

These three deities, Sampo Kojin, Zao Gongen and Sanmen Daikokuten, are the real gods of good monetary fortune in the righteous spirit world and they cause absolutely no harm. Moreover, they are "Made in Japan" Buddhas who are prepared without fail to bestow on you unexcelled spiritual power.

At present my companies are operating through a symbiosis of the principles of *shin*, *soe* and *hikae*. Consequently, we are enjoying astonishing expansion of our sales network, spectacular growth of sales, steadily climbing profit ratios and total elimination of debts.

In fact, our worries now center around how much taxes we will be required to pay at the end of the business year.

But we always try to bear in mind that the fact that the basic reason the company is now progressing on an even keel and enjoying the full support of the divine world is entirely a result of the fact that we paid our tough dues for so long way back when.

To be more specific, at the beginning of the month *shin* and *soe* work together to drive the business forward, while towards the end of the month *hikae* tidies up the accounts. Although other methods are involved in the case of large business enterprises, for individuals or small companies such as I run, this is the best way to proceed. My company World Mate also sells images of these three deities. I can assure you that worshipping in the fashion I have just described is the key to receiving the proper form of good luck with money from the divine world.

It goes without saying that should your prayers be answered and you are granted good luck with money from the spirit world, you should fully express your feelings of gratitude to the gods. Thank these gods of *shinsoehikae* from the bottom of your heart.

Three Factors Required for Real Results

In any age it is difficult for a businessman to be successful at his profession and keep his profits steadily rising. He no doubt has many rivals, and he has no way of knowing whether he will be able to continue to satisfy all his customers, or whether and if so when they might switch to a competitor.

Maybe it is because of the many uncertain factors that affect their daily lives. But it seems to me that many businessmen and entrepreneurs actively worship the gods and Buddhas. Even if that is a bit of an exaggeration, there is no denying that people in business tend to be superstitious. For that reason you will often find small shrines on the top of office buildings and it only seems natural when you spot a "god shelf" in a company president's office.

These are good instances of how to go about praying for divine aid. I simply will not do to drop your head and mumble a few words. For a businessman, or anyone for that matter, the important thing is to live the way he should, in other words do his best at all times. If he does that and also prays to the gods and Buddhas with a pure heart, then he will surely receive their protection and support.

If you forget these things and merely fold your hands together and pray, "Oh, sacred gods and Buddhas, let my business prosper," such conduct will probably have absolutely no effect. Such an approach might work with low level spirits or Inari foxes, but it will leave the true deities of the righteous spirit world unconvinced.

The key to making your business flourish – besides of course efficiently handling various day-to-day problems like labor relations and ordering necessary materials – is to pursue your business activities in a pure and simple fashion, in accordance with the following three points:

1. Raising sales (through your efforts to introduce new products or acquire new customers);

2. Cutting business expenses (through elimination of waste and maximization of profit);

3. Ensuring collections (in other words, regularizing your cash flow). No doubt many of the managers reading this book may be grumbling to themselves, "Well those things are pretty obvious, aren't they?"

But I can assure you, if you take a close look at businesses that are having trouble boosting their profits, you are certain to find that they are failing in regard to at least one of these three critical factors. And businessmen who are famous for their ability to turn companies around through restructuring are well aware of the importance of these three key elements. Your typical manager is often in trouble on all three scores at the same time.

In the first case, you will often find companies that are skillfully able to increase their sales, but are spending too much on superfluous things, make too many sales on credit, and cannot seem to make their collections within time limits. This sometimes results in the phenomenon known as "bankruptcy while in the black." In other words, although a company's ledgers may be running a surplus, because of a shortage of funds the firm goes under. A "bankruptcy while in the black" occurs because of cash flow problems.

Conversely, in the case of the second point, even should a company drastically cut costs, if the essential sales are just not there, then the firm is heading for its downfall.

Finally, we come to the problem of cash flow. As I am sure any of you who are involved in the management of a business are well aware, this can be a real headache. Things are not so bad when sales are made on a cash basis. But when the merchandise is turned over to the customer beforehand and payment is made sometime later, or even more so in the worst cases when payment is dragged out over a long period of time or compensation for labor is made two to three weeks after the service is performed, businessmen cannot afford to remain optimistic.

They are always aware of the fact that a customer could go bankrupt at any time, likely leaving their IOUs uncollectable. It is not at all uncommon to encounter companies that look good in their books, but do not have a cent in their cash box.

I hope I have made clear just how important these three conditions are for a business. The same principles also operate at the personal level. Increases in sales are the equivalent of the amount of work done and size of the paycheck for a worker. Trimming business expenses is the same as keeping a close watch on luxuries in the family budget. And of course cash flow – how much comes in and how much goes out – is of the utmost importance to every home as well as every business.

Just to give a few specific examples in this regard, we should take steps to make sure that we do not overpay taxes and maximize our use of available capital. Furthermore, we need to refrain from using precious savings to invest in dubious stocks or futures speculation, and give careful consideration to all the implications of inheritance taxes.

The Wise God Zao Gongen

In order to increase sales, you need a sharp brain and relentless determination. In order to develop a new product that will take the market by storm and leave your competitors reeling, first of all you have to carry out an accurate analysis of market conditions and your possible sales outlets. You need a combination of a good idea, a touch of genius and wisdom.

Zao Gongen is the deity in charge of the practical wisdom needed to make it in the world. So he is the one to whom you should address your appeals for assistance.

O mighty Zao Gongen, you who possess all worldly wisdom. Please endow me with the wisdom needed so that our sales will skyrocket. Of course, I also promise to work as hard as possible. Take into consideration my efforts and then please grant me the profound genius and wisdom I require. I entreat you.

This is the kind of prayer you need to offer. But it goes without saying that when you pray to Zao Gongen, you cannot do so with a selfish or jealous heart. While asking for benefits for yourself, you should also wish well for others.

Incidentally, Zao Gongen is the smartest being anywhere around in the material world. And his power will always achieve its purpose in the end, despite any opposition. He is a true "Made in Japan" Buddha, who first appeared on Mt. Omine, when the Nara era monk Enno Ozune, founder of the shugendo regimen of esoteric

蔵王権現

Buddhism, was there practicing austerities.

Say you have an important business meeting tomorrow and you need to overwhelm the person you are meeting with your knowledge. In such a case, make sure before you leave for the conference you whisper a little prayer to Zao Gongen.

Sampo Kojin

The next deity we are going to look at is Sampo Kojin. He is the one who handles the second factor, the cutting of expenses to increase profits. Sampo Kojin is also honored in the average home as the Kitchen God.

Sampo Kojin also first appeared to Enno Ozune when he was undergoing his arduous devotions on Mt. Omine. This is how the encounter came about. One day when Ennozune was engaged in his spiritual training, without warning a violent earthquake shook the earth beneath him. Then the holy man noticed a very strange cloud off to the northeast. When he approached it, he saw that it was the god Sampo Kojin, who spoke to him as follows:

I am the god of the nine mountains and nine rivers in this area, who will aid those engaged in a spiritual quest.

In other words, the god was telling Enno Ozune that besides bestowing good luck with money, he, Sampo Kojin would reward those who gave their all in spiritual training and endeavors.

If we explain this in terms of human relations, Sampo Kojin was declaring that he was a being of honor who would fulfill his obligations. That is why, even if your family does not enjoy much wealth, because of the evil karmic influence of actions by your ancestors, you should pray to this deity, while working just as hard as you can. You can rest assured that you will surely be rewarded for those efforts.

三宝荒神

Originally, Sampo Kojin took the form of Kuni-toko-dachi-no-mikoto, who is the source of the power of the earth. This deity, mentioned in the *Kojiki*, hid gentleness underneath a rough exterior. If you are a businessman who is in the position where you have to eliminate reckless management and ruthlessly cut business costs or have to deal with similar problems, then Sampo Kojin can help you act most efficiently.

Sampo Kojin is as I have pointed out the Kitchen God, who helps families to keep firm control of the monthly budget. If you worship him properly, then he will reward you with good luck in making ends meet. You should do so in a kitchen or other place with a flame and water.

The reason is that one of the readings in Japanese for the Chinese character for "fire" is *ka* and likewise a reading for the character for "water" is *mi*. Together these are read as *kami*, or "god." In other words, when these two elements are present, the god Sampo Kojin can best exhibit his power. I explain the correct way to worship this deity later in the book.

Back when Kukai was first building his religious center on Mt. Koya, the construction was continuously interrupted by storms. In response, he undertook rigorous spiritual training. One day while so engaged, the nearby mountains rumbled and Sampo Kojin appeared to him. After that the construction proceeded smoothly and was completed without a hitch. In effect, Sambo Kojin acted as the sponsor for the project. He is a god who truly takes care of those who place their faith in him.

The kitchen is one of the most important rooms in the daily life of any family. If you worship Sampo Kojin here, then he will make sure that your family finances do not get out of hand and that you enjoy good fortune. I urge you to pray to him with all sincerity.

Moreover, to you businessmen I say: if you fold your hands, bow your head and pray in front of his kitchen shrine without fail every single day, I guarantee that you can expect to see your profits soar miraculously.

Another thing to remember is that when you pray for something, be as specific as possible. Let me give you an example:

"On such and such a date, at such and such a time, I have an important business meeting with Mr. X. I need to close a deal with him worth at least this many dollars. I pray that somehow you will fix things so as to make Mr. X happy and have the meeting come out entirely to my satisfaction."

That is the way to do it. In my book Lucky Fortune, I also explain the proper way to ask your guardian spirits for help. The situation is basically the same with Sampo Kojin: the more detailed the request, the more likely it is that you will get him working for you. Which is to say that just like the guardian spirits, Sampo Kojin is always in close proximity to people. His existence is sheer power, and in a form that is a good deal more friendly than that of employees at your local tax office, tax accountants or business accountants. Make sure you approach him in the correct fashion.

I should add that Sampo Kojin has six arms, two legs and three faces. As you can well imagine from this description, he is a multi-talented, "can-do" type of kami.

Sanmen Daikokuten

As I explained earlier, good fortune with money is something that is passed on from one person to another. For example, in businesses where you are dealing directly with clients, good contacts mean good opportunities for making money. The job of the third member

of the divine trio we have been considering, Sanmen Daikokuten, is to create opportunities for you to meet people loaded with monetary fortune or influential individuals who can advance your career and help bring you lots more customers. So you can see, he is a very good deity to get to know.

Sanmen Daikokuten appeared to Saicho when he was busy on Mt. Hiei seeking to establish it as the base for the Tendai school. He was praying wholeheartedly at the time. The god's appearance was designed to help Saicho establish contacts and recruit men of great talent. In other words, draw the right kind of people to himself. In fact, Sanmen Daikokuten's help proved invaluable in bringing many Buddhist priests to Mt. Hiei and helping the Enryakuji Temple to flourish as perhaps the most important center of Buddhism in all Japan.

And the implacable power that kept Saint Nichiren going against all odds too was a gift from Sanmen Daikokuten. This is how it came about. When Nichiren first began preaching the superiority of the Lotus Sutra, no one paid him any attention. So Nichiren said to himself, "Why is it that no one will pay heed to my preaching? We are now in *Mappo*, the age of decline and decadence, and if the people do not learn to place their faith in the Lotus Sutra, they cannot be saved."

He was troubled as to what he should do under these circumstances. Just at that point, Sanmen Daikokuten took note of his spiritual suffering and used his spiritual power to attract many people to Nichiren. In other words, this god helps individuals when they are in a bind by bringing others who have the power or resources to help them out to them. That was shown in the case of Nichiren when he prayed fervently for the gods' help in disseminating the message of the Lotus Sutra.

What characterizes the way the god works is that he helps create a web of relations among people, so that each can borrow from the strength of others. Viewed on the spiritual level, he is a manifestation of the brilliantly gold Kanzeon Bosatsu, or Goddess of Mercy. In addition, in his normal form he has three faces, as distinct from regular Daikokuten gods of fortune that have only one. That is because his power is so much greater.

Daikokuten

At the same time Daikokuten carries a big bag. That is so he can whisk away calamities affecting people and at the same time distribute to them happiness and prosperity. In other words, he is something like a cross between your scrap metal recycling man and Santa Claus. And he often also gives transfusions of good luck to people who are suffering from severe fortune anemia.

But this god is not engaged merely in such charitable activities. Be aware that in his right hand he tightly grips a mallet. Although Daikokuten is always prepared to help those who deserve it, he refuses to give one iota of good fortune to lazy people unless preconditions are met. That is why he carries the mallet, to give the lazy a whack or two on the head.

Try a little harder! Put out! Good fortune is just beyond your grasp. But if you're going to malinger, you deserve a taste of this!

If you really listen, you can hear Daikokuten talking in this way to you. So when you are troubled or suffering, just remember that he is right nearby you, waiting to provide you with good fortune. The trick is to have faith and keep on trying.

Daikokuten can be compared to the "big black pillar" or central foundation pillar of a traditional Japanese home. In normal times he is as steady and predictable as a rock. But when he moves into action, he is dynamite. In order to make it easier for him to help you out at such times, make sure to make offerings of water and rice at his shrine in your home. Water, in other words "moisture," is identified with the northern direction and the zodiacal sign of the rat. So a rat serves as Daikokuten's helper and as his messenger.

As you know water, dampness or moisture can change form and flow into any space. This is also exactly the way that the movement of good fortune from Daikokuten operates when the ring of good fortune expands to link more and more people together. So you can see why water and Daikokuten are related. He is also considered the god of the five grains, which are symbolically represented by rice. In other words, the five grains also symbolize development and fertility.

Unify Yourself for Better Fortune

As I explained earlier, spiritually a human being has one soul composed of four distinct spirits. And Zao Gongen, Sampo Kojin and Sanmen Daikokuten each fortifies one of these spirits.

For instance, Zao Gongen backs up the wisdom faculty, or *kushimitama*. His presence is also essential for developing successful management or entrepreneurial strategies. This is also the deity who will help you boost your sales and encourage you to return unneeded merchandise.

Sampo Kojin is a fierce and courageous deity, who influences the *aramitama* that gives a person the resoluteness that he or she requires. Since this character asset is tied directly to the ability to manage family finances or cut operating costs in connection with accounting, it is not surprising to find that the presence of this god

113

is a must when you have to hold the line and not give an inch. He can stiffen your resolve when you most need it, as for example when you are negotiating for price increases.

Then we have the *sakimitama*, the spirit of love and happiness. The *nigimitama*, the spirit of harmony. It is assuredly attuned to the spiritual vibrations given off by the rotund, jovial Sanmen Daikokuten, whose beaming face is a clear invitation to business prosperity. He can cause customers to come running.

The *kushimitama, nigimitama, aramitama* and *sakimitama* together constitute the soul. So if a person can express the full power of the four distinct parts of his or her soul with the assistance of these divine spirits, then he or she will have gained enormous spiritual power that will help make possible the realization of the dream of good fortune in money affairs.

Now, I should emphasize that it is important to pray to these three deities every single day, and to do so in specific terms and in the correct fashion. Think of it as something like a booster shot of spiritual vitamins. Even a small dose can have a huge effect. The important thing is to make it a daily routine.

Getting the Most out of Divine Help

Among my readers who have read faithfully up to this point, I am sure there are some people whose eyebrows are raised and who are saying things like this to themselves, "Is he for real with all this jazz about Sampo Kojin, Sanmen Daikokuten or whomever. If it was really so easy to win divine favor when it comes to making money, then why is my life in such a mess. Things aren't that easy in the real world. All you really get is blood, sweat and tears."

Some of the things I have written may indeed seem unbelievable to people who have experienced failure on many occasions and who harbor bitter memories. But I assure you, every word I write is true.

Chances for good luck come everyone's way. And we all have times when we are run ragged trying to raise money. It is at such times that you need to display your full talents and spiritual power.

There seems to be a pattern in the way people fail to grab their chance at fortune. Just when the chance is sitting there in front of them and they should be exerting their everything, they get cold feet. They tell themselves things like: "Ah, it's no use. I never stand a chance. My luck was out to lunch from day one. Give my all and I'll end up with next to nothing to show for it. Better to just give as much as I need to get by and not tire myself out."

With such a half-hearted, spineless attitude is it any wonder that such people inevitably fail? My goodness, they are already half-beaten before they even start. And if they keep thinking like that, they will never get anywhere for all eternity.

In other words, if you have a negative image of yourself to start with, you are going to end up finding yourself in the spiritual realm of defeat. If that happens, no matter how much you wish and wish for good luck with money, according to the pattern that has been proven on countless occasions, you will not be able to get the gods working for you.

But on the other hand, if no matter how much suffering you might experience and what depths of poverty you plummet to, you never waver in your belief that: "I'm going to win for sure. If I just hang in there, I am certain to be rewarded in the end. I'm positive I'm destined to be super-lucky." And you act in accordance with this belief. Then the gods are sure to take note and good fortune will come flying to you.

Even if objectively he has failed, the wise man looks upon this failure as the seed of future successes. He is confident that it will in fact invite good fortune. The most important thing here is that he adopt the right frame of mind and emotional state. Furthermore, if he is praying to the gods and Buddhas daily, then the ideas that he is producing are of a quality that can quickly be transformed into positive factors working for him.

In effect, such a person who prays to the gods, believes in himself and does his best in his everyday life has already created the conditions that in the realm of thought beckons good fortune and induces the deities to lend their protective support.

Consequently, if you pray to the three gods whom I have just introduced, you should bear in mind the importance of firm belief in these fundamental principles. If you fold your hands and mumble your prayers half in jest, then your requests for wealth will violate taboos. Of course, the gods are not so mean-hearted that they are going to order divine retribution down on your head for your less than serious prayers. But if evil spirits catch wind of such prayers, they are likely to show up at your door and are capable of doing just about anything. One thing you can be sure of, the results will not be pleasant.

In order to take full advantage of the power of the three gods of good fortune, you need to have firm faith, pray daily, activate positive thoughts and seek to make them reality. If you do all these things conscientiously, then you will reinforce by many times your own spiritual power and the influence of the power you borrow from the three gods of good fortune should increase by ten-fold. And it is best that you make such a program of action second nature to you.

Trust the Gods and Fear Nothing

The gods are firm allies of common people like ourselves. That is especially true of the Three Gods of Monetary Fortune, who are always in close proximity to us and whose collective presence therefore is intimately related to our daily lives. So discard here and now any misguided thinking you may have that the gods should only be worshipped in times of need. Instead try to think of these three gods in more intimate terms, as being friends who are with you every single moment.

Now let me give you some advice on how you can get to know these three gods well.

First of all remember that the beginning of the month belongs to Sanmen Daikokuten. The reason for that is that this is the period when you want to bring a lot of people together and expand business greatly.

The middle of the month on the other hand is the period when you should concentrate your petitions to Zao Gongen. That is because now you want to take full advantage of your intellect and find ways to accumulate money and increase sales.

And the end of the month, of course, is the period when you have to make payments and balance your company's ledgers. You have to deal with lots of troublesome figures and can expect to be facing off with hordes of bill collectors. Now is the time when you need the courage, resoluteness and fierceness that Sampo Kojin has an ample supply of. You can borrow from his strength to help you ride out skillfully this perilous period at the end of the month.

If you begin to think like this, then you will understand how the conduct of these three gods, who have such a big impact on the way the soul and its four constituent spirits interact, is part and parcel of the daily life of the common man.

Furthermore, if you want to make your way in the world by creating associations with others and attracting good fortune, you should concentrate your thoughts in these regards around the image of Sanmen Daikokuten. The same thing holds true for Sampo Kojin if you want to refine your personality, force yourself to deal more dynamically with others and actively develop your capabilities and thus get ahead in business. Or Zao Gongen if you wish to draw fully on your supply of wisdom or develop things in a theoretical way.

Just think of such strategies as a temporary expedient. There is no need to get too uptight about it. What you are actually doing is applying in utilitarian fashion the fundamental principles of *shin, soe, hikae* that I explained earlier. Take things on a case-by-case, experimental basis. The important thing is that you achieve personal understanding and experience. Remember, the various secret techniques for acquiring good luck I will introduce later in this book derive their excellence from these basic forms and applications.

The Seven Divinities of Good Luck

Gods of Old Japan Foster Our Growth

These days even teeny boppers know the names of the Seven Divinities of Good Luck. They are as I noted earlier: Bishamonten, Ebisu, Daikokuten, Fukurokuju, Jurojin, Benzai Tennyo and Hotei Osho. The origins of these seven divinities are diverse. Fukurokuju and Jurojin, for example, were borrowed from Taoism. They are also sometimes referred to as *spirits of the South Pole*. Benzaiten and Daikokuten on the other hand were adopted from esoteric sects

of Buddhism. Ebisu is the refined form of a native Japanese god who had been extremely popular from ancient times among the common people because of his ability to ensure good fishing.

And as for Bishamonten, he is alternatively known as Vaisravana, the god of treasure, and Tamonten, one of the four heavenly kings. As such he is one of the military gods of Buddhism, whose assignment it is to protect the kitchen, and by extension finances. The last of the seven, Hotei Osho, is said to be derived from a historical person, a mendicant priest who once lived in China.

Here again I will get into a more detailed explanation of each of these divinities a bit later on, but here suffice it to say that these particular divinities seem to epitomize divine characteristics more than human characteristics. Furthermore, their original nationalities vary, as do the sects and even religions from which these gods originally appeared. But somehow or other in popular representations they all ended up as one merry crew on the same "Treasure Boat."

No doubt, Christians, Jews or other believers in a monotheistic religion will have their socks knocked off with surprise when they realize what is happening here.

But you have to bear in mind that the Japanese people are notoriously promiscuous when it comes to religion. At New Year, they invariably visit a Shinto shrine. But many get married in a Christian ceremony and have a Buddhist funeral for their kin.

Their attitude seems to be: "It's really the same divine power providing happiness, so if your feelings are pure, what does it matter what form your worship assumes." Actually, this is really a magnanimous way of thinking. But the backbone rationale that underlies this way of thought is nothing other than the spirit of Japan's ancient native religion of Shinto.

Over 1,500 years ago, when Buddhism was first introduced into Japan, a bit of a struggle developed between those who wanted to welcome the foreign religion and those who rejected it. Eventually, it was decided to allow Buddhism and Shinto to coexist. And then later in Japanese history, although there were occasions on which Christianity was suppressed and Buddhism was persecuted, in general a spirit of tolerance held sway and many aspects of these religions too were incorporated into the daily lives of the Japanese. In that sense, the Japanese can be said to be a very unusual people.

Concepts like the Seven Divinities of Good Luck are in many ways very Japanese and very Shinto-like. The good side of the original beliefs was accepted and blended. Such an open, tolerant method of receiving new ideas is really superbly rational.

From the point of view of the divine world, if a person believes, it is really not very important what his or her nationality, skin color, sex or age is. After all, the gods themselves never, never bad mouth each other or fight.

Well, now that we are finished with this long introduction, let me point out that the present lineup of the Seven Divinities of Good Luck was already in place as far back as the middle of the Muromachi Period (1338-1573) and many Japanese were praying to them then. And even today, it is apparent from the way that many people fervently pray to them that these deities are truly capable of bringing advantage to their devotees.

Bishamonten

The member of the magnificent seven with the sternest countenance is undoubtedly Bishamonten. Under the alternative name of Tamonten, he is counted as one of the Four Heavenly

Kings. He is also the military god charged with defense of the northern direction. Despite his intimidating bearing, and perhaps for the reason that his skin color is yellow – just like us – the Japanese feel a particular affinity for this deity.

However, it would be a mistake to believe that right from the start Bishamonten was on the side of good and a defender of humankind. Quite the opposite, actually. Rather, he was a strong-armed thug in the spirit world, who also tested the limits of iniquity in the material world, riding roughshod over everyone, pillaging, raping, murdering and quarreling.

Then one day he ran into the Lord Buddha, Shakyamuni, and received his teaching.

Even if you hate others and torment them, you will find no sense of satisfaction in your heart. It is not in reducing others to grief and tears that you will find fulfillment but in viewing their faces overflowing with happiness.

After he had accepted the Buddha's message, Bishamonten underwent a complete change of heart and became a deity of good who has ever since used his immense power to help others. This story of transformation from the epitome of evil to good is almost exactly like the story of Kishimojin, the guardian deity of children.

As her name suggests when written in Chinese characters, Kishimojin was a mother monster who had an insatiable appetite for eating other people's children. Any child or infant that she got her hands on soon ended up in her stomach. Even when she saw the mothers of these children howling in despair, she would just grin malevolently.

But that situation did not continue endlessly. It got to the point where the Buddha would no longer put up with this carnage on the part of Kishimojin, who showed no inclination to repent her countless evil deeds. So what he did was get a hold of her own children and hide them away. When she discovered that her own beloved offspring had disappeared, Kishimojin was driven to distraction with worry.

She went mad with grief and wept tears of blood. As a result, she suddenly realized the full horror of her sins of eating babies and could finally fathom the unbearable sorrow that gripped the hearts of their mothers. She underwent a total conversion on the spot, and thereafter became the protective deity for children.

In the cases of both Bishamonten and Kishimojin, it was only after they had tasted the dregs of evil and repented that they could give full rein to their stupendous power. Moreover, since they are well acquainted with the ways of evil, they have the strength to conquer it. In fact, these gods prefer not to wait and defend against the forces of evil. Instead they take the offensive and seek them out to subjugate and exterminate them. They might be compared to Superman or the Lone Ranger.

Bishamonten in particular, his being a military god, finds his very raison d'être in routing evil and promoting good. In today's society, where you no doubt have any number of rivals, it is advisable to rely on Bishamonten's power for good luck. In the past, several famous warriors, including the 16th century warlord Uesugi Kenshin and the famous royalist hero Kusunoki Masashige, relied on Bishamonten as their protective deity and were thus able to make a name for themselves.

Now here I would like to make another little digression and explain the difference in the Buddhist variety of power best represented by Bishamonten and the Shinto type of power embodied in the Sun Goddess Ama-terasu-o-mikami.

In Buddhism, take for example the Nichiren chant *Namu Myoho*

Rengekyo ("Glory to the Sutra of the Lotus of the Supreme Law"), the emphasis is on keeping a strict guard up against evil.

Never be defeated by evil! Such a battle cry always seems to be on the lips of the truly devout Buddhist. That is no doubt due at least in part to the personal history of Shakyamuni. After all, it was only after he had drunk deeply from the cup of luxury that he could reject temptation and attain the state of enlightenment. From his earliest days as a prince he had had the opportunity to observe and understand human beings from all strata of society.

I should also note that up until now I have been able to evaluate many, many different guardian spirits, and among their ranks there seem to be an inordinately large number of Buddhist spirits identified with the Nichiren sect. Many of these guardian spirits are the ancestors from a dozen or so generations back of the person they are protecting. But that does not mean that just anyone can become a guardian spirit. Just as in our society only those elite few who can pass national civil service exams for government agencies, the foreign service or the bar exam can expect to qualify for certain positions, in the spirit world as well, a candidate wishing to be appointed as a guardian spirit has to pass a quite difficult examination.

As you can tell just by the job title *guardian spirit*, the spirit in question must possess power sufficient to ward off evil from his charge. For that reason, he had to be fighting against evil even while he was alive and then continued that crusade after dying and entering the spirit world.

When Nichiren achieved enlightenment on a beach skirting Tokyo Bay, while looking into the rising sun, the chant *Namu Myoho Rengekyo* came spontaneously to his lips. The power he displayed at that moment was exactly the kind of power needed by a guardian spirit.

Just for your reference, if you take a close look at the ranks of the guardian spirits, you will find that priests belonging to the Nichiren sect are far and away in first place numberwise, followed by Zen priests, *samurai* and village headmen. Christians can also be found. But the type of power that allows a spirit to stand up to evil and set the person who is being protected on the right path is really only to be found among spirits with a Buddhist background.

Then we have Shinto. Here we have to look at things from a different dimension, unrelated to the question of how powerful or weak something is standing up to evil. You might say that the basic message of Shinto is to *have enthusiasm, and to live a happy, positive life*.

Consequently, Shinto is not very interested in searching out evil and it does not emphasize the concepts of sin or punishment. For example, in Shinto you never hear expressions like, *We human beings wallow in a sea of sin. We must repent at once.*

Rather the accent in Shinto is on moving ahead with life.

Actually, if we are honest we will have to admit that compared to Buddhism, Shinto's guard against evil is very weak. That is certainly one of its defects. However, we should also highly appraise its emphasis on cheerfully looking towards the future. The power created by such an attitude is absolutely essential for spreading good.

As I already explained in *Lucky Fortune*, Buddhism equates with the spirit world of the moon, while Shinto equates with the spirit world of the sun. They are in fact the manifestations of these two worlds in our material world. The moon of course shines at night, and in this case faintly illuminates the evil aspects of humankind.

The sun, on the other hand, bathes the world in radiant light and lends life to the plants, trees and animals. From the perspective of the sun, night represents the reverse side of the earth, in other words the part that is not visible. Actually when this night side of the earth is viewed directly, this side too is faintly visible – in the reflected glow of the moon.

Anyway, as you can see, Shinto power is directed towards having a bright, forward-looking life, while Buddhist power is obsessed with seeking out and conquering all evil inside and outside a person's heart. But isn't a combination of the two really the ideal? I believe so, and that is the reason I work so hard to achieve a healthy working relationship between the two religions.

Benzaiten

Veneration of Benzaiten as the god who invites in good fortune with money even now is quite strong among the common people in Japan. You have to give the common man credit for his sharp eye for the truth. If no advantage is to be gained, there is no reason for any form of popular belief to last over the generations.

The three most important Benten images worshipped in Japan are located at Itsukushima near Hiroshima, Chikubujima in Lake Biwa and at Enoshima near Tokyo. But the Benten at Tenkawa in the Kansai district of Western Japan might be considered the "boss" of these various Benten.

A close look at the Chinese characters for Benzaiten reveals something interesting. *Zai* means "treasure" or "wealth." That shows just what a deep connection Benzaiten has with wealth. In other words, the whole background of this god is intimately tied to the idea of wealth and good fortune.

Benzaiten is a female deity. Her ultimate forerunners were a trio of goddesses who appeared from the sword of the Storm God Susa-no-o-no-mikoto. Since a sword is used to cut things and thereby multiply the parts, it is frequently used as a symbol for economics and riches. Since the sword equals wealth, the three deities born from Susa-no-o-no-mikoto's sword – Tagori Hime, Tagiri Hime and Tagitsu Hime – have miraculous powers when it comes to things to do with wealth.

Also, perhaps because Benzaiten is a female, this deity is extremely charming. Images of Benzaiten, such as the one at Enoshima, often depict her stark naked, with her ample busts protruding and a *biwa* lute that can bring the sweetest of music to human ears lying in her lap. The loving, powerful spiritual vibrations given off by the goddess are unequaled when it comes to being able to fulfill the wishes of male worshippers desiring to get ahead in the world and to enjoy good luck with money. Of course, the same holds true for female worshippers.

At first thought, you might doubt the connection between attractiveness and good fortune. You might even think I am all wet in this connection. But I assure you that people who make it in life and attain wealth are almost without exception charming individuals. You seldom hear about an ugly, loathsome creature who never has a pleasing smile for others enjoying good fortune.

And I also guarantee you that in the future bosses and superiors will tend to be appointed from the ranks of people who can gain the trust of others through their affability, rather than people who rely on sheer, unrefined skill. Thus, as you can see, a pleasing disposition can be a major weapon in getting ahead and making money.

A good example of a person who used his charm to make the world his oyster was Toyotomi Hideyoshi, the de facto ruler of Japan in the late 16th century.

And humor is the same skill when viewed from a different angle. Ronald Reagan, for example, when president of the United States was a genius when it came to telling jokes. Of course, he also was a skilled politician. His combination of skills helped him get to the top. In the case of Japan, many prominent politicians, including former prime minister Kakuei Tanaka, have been known for their sense of humor.

The *ben* in Benzaiten also has a special meaning, namely eloquence in speaking or argument. For that reason, people who would rely on their linguistic or persuasive powers to get ahead would be well advised to worship the goddess. When you can combine these two qualities of *ben* and *zai*, that is when you will really see things go your way. In the cold society of today, the man who can win the trust of others because of his talking ability and sense of humor has the inside track on getting ahead and making his fortune even if he does not have any other special skills.

If we take a look at this from the viewpoint of the soul and its four constituent spirits, we can see that pleasantness of personality is a characteristic of the *nigimitama* that corresponds with the virtue of harmony. As I explained earlier, Bishamonten represents fierce courage and resoluteness, characteristics of the *aramitama*.

The ideal, of course, is to be able to combine smoothly this with the harmony we have just been discussing. If you can do that, you are already a long way towards making your fortune. You will be able to display in appropriate degrees pluck and sweetness, the sheer power of the male and the soft mood of the female.

Ebisu

Next, let's take a look at Ebisu.

This name can be written with several different Chinese characters or combinations of Chinese characters. For example, one means "warning" and another means "foreign." As these indicate, this deity originally hailed from overseas and is always on his guard against danger.

The famous statue of Ebisu at Nishinomiya in Kansai appears to be slightly hard of hearing. So worshippers who come to plead for success in business go around to the back of the shrine, knock on the door and call out in a loud voice things like: "Oh, Great Ebisu. I am Joe Tanaka living in Osaka. Today, January 10, on this festival day sacred to you, I come to ask your continued favor in the year ahead."

All of these things are really references to making wealth. Bamboo grass flowers only once every sixty years, so it has an image of great patience and fortitude. In other words, these prayers are using the image of the bamboo grass to beg Ebisu for good luck with money.

Nevertheless, you would be sorely mistaken if you concluded that these were nothing but a bunch of empty words strung together.

The god Ebisu is depicted as carrying a fishing rod and cradling a huge sea bream in his arm. Such fish are by no means easy to catch. No matter how skilled a fisherman may be, he must patiently stalk such a catch for days on end, if he hopes to have any success. He has to remain unflappable and be willing to release with a smile any small fry that may come along and just wait and wait until he catches that special bream. It is only the truly expert fisherman who has the confidence and patience to do this right.

The smile on Ebisu's face has this lesson for us: You have to have strong self-confidence and the willingness to bide your time patiently without allowing your smile to fade. In fact, although popular rumor may have it that the Ebisu at Nishinomiya is hard of hearing, that is not true at all. The Ebisu there can hear perfectly what people are saying. Nevertheless, he pretends to be hard of hearing. He is willing to ignore any weird talk, pretending that it never reached his ears. This behavior is proof of the fine character of this provider of prosperity and bearer of good fortune.

A salesman I know who works for a major office machines equipment manufacturer has discovered the Ebisu way for making it big in the world. I would like to share a bit of his story with you.

At one time he was a businessman in the middle ranks of management at his company. But somehow he found he just could not advance; he could not manage to take that one extra little step to the big time.

However, after hearing about the Ebisu method of success, he decided that his sales strategy had been wrong. So instead of continuing to concentrate on small shops and businesses like he had up till then, he went straight to the biggest boys – top purchasers of office equipment. This despite the fact that he had absolutely no connections among them.

At the beginning doors slammed in his face regularly and such put downs as "We don't need you guys" rang in his ears. But just like the Nishinomiya Ebisu, he would act like he had not heard a word of rejection. He just kept doing the best he could.

Finally a department chief from one of these companies said to him one day, "You're really something else. Everyday you're out there hustling and that really impresses me. We're considering ordering a new office automation system, and I'll tell you what, I

think we'll give your stuff a try in our section."

This success served as his entrée, and pretty soon he had orders from all the departments in that mammoth firm. This success in getting his company's equipment ordered was nothing less than a business coup. And acceptance by a major client had a tremendous ripple affect.

When his marketing strategy had concentrated on small shops and businesses, repeat orders were few and far between. But now he was dealing with a major manufacturer. And the integrated production and other connections tying that firm to affiliated companies and cooperating production plants meant that he could start selling the same system to these other places as well. So by following the Ebisu way, this salesman was able to land a very big "sea bream."

And it goes without saying that every day during that wait he had folded his hands and prayed to Ebisu for success in the business wars.

Anyone can set their goals for things that can be easily accomplished. But not many people will dare to try for that which appears impossible. So that is what you should be aiming for. Still that does not mean that it is going to be easy. Far from it. You have to be prepared to stick it out for the long haul if you want to land that giant sea bream. That is the Ebisu-style business strategy.

The reason that the shrine at Nishinomiya uses the Chinese character meaning "warning" for the name Ebisu is that it is really a form of advice to worshippers. That is, if you want to really, really succeed in business, you have to control yourself and your ego and be prepared to persevere. The spirit of kind Ebisu is enshrined here, so the name certainly is not intended to discourage worship.

Jurojin

Jurojin has a head that is elongated to the point of bizarrity. He is also totally bald. A manifestation of the god of one of the stars in the southern skies, Canopus, Jurojin is also extremely clever. Canopus is the second brightest star in the firmament and as such can be seen faintly even from Tokyo on a clear summer's night. But a lot of luck is required here, because it sits at an angle only two degrees above the horizon. However, Jurojin's head is so big and long not just because he has a lot of brains to be packed in. No, as the saying *The limbs that bear most hang lowest* makes clear, a drooping head is an important sign. A person who knows that he is extremely bright is liable to keep his nose up in the air and treat everyone around him like an idiot. And that can in no way be considered the proper way to act.

The wiser a man is, the more likely he is to adopt a low profile or to even slouch in his attempt to avoid attention. These are the manners of the truly wise. This humility of the wise man is also closely tied to the humility we should show in our daily lives – in simplicity of living and the importance of being thrifty. That is the reason that Jurojin is considered as the god of thrift. He has refined this virtue to a fine art, rationally searching out every possible method for saving money.

In general society too we can see how this principle operates. Virtuous elderly people live humble, simple lives, making sure to eat every last grain of rice in their rice bowls for example. They also nurture grateful hearts. Such an attitude beckons good fortune and keeps it sitting complacently outside your door.

Many times when a person is brilliant, talented and loaded with money, he or she also tends to be highly conceited. Individuals who tend to be that way should work with Jurojin in seeking to control their own faults.

Fukurokuju

Just like Jurojin, Fukurokuju is also a manifestation of the god of the star Canopus. In fact they are often equated, which is no big problem since their spiritual power tends to express itself in the same ways.

But while Jurojin teaches us the importance of being humble, Fukurokuju reveals to us the importance of thinking correctly. By thinking, we mean the ability to carefully ruminate about your ideas until they mature and to take into account the opinions of others.

Here I should point out that if we rely simply on our own intelligence, then our knowledge is going to be severely limited. When you get several people together, then you can start drawing on the collective wisdom. This is truly a case of the more the merrier, since it is only from this pool of ideas that true wisdom can emerge.

In other words, if you are not willing to listen to other people, then you really have very little chance to have your talent recognized and to become rich. You do not even stand much chance of developing any original ideas. The truly intelligent man acts humble and skillfully draws on the thinking of other people. They do not go brazenly strutting around, doing things their own way.

If someone obviously has talent but cannot seem to get ahead, then more often than not you will find that this wrong attitude is the cause of their failure. A talented man who would be humble and open to the opinions of others, or he would become brilliant but prudent, or quick thinking, should direct his prayers to Fukurokuju.

The ruling deity of the North Pole spiritual world, an ancient named Taiotsu, also is a god of great wisdom. So you can also direct the same kind of prayers to him. For further details, kindly consult *Lucky Fortune*.

Hotei Osho

The only one of the Seven Divinities of Good Luck who was originally a human being is Hotei Osho. The other six hailed from the spirit world to begin with. According to tradition, he was a mendicant priest, who wandered around China many centuries ago. Eventually, he came to be revered by others as the Maitreya bodhisattva, who indeed he was in human form. But although he gave off the spiritual energy waves of a bodhisattva, his physical appearance belied his spiritual power, since he was bald as an eagle and had a grotesquely roly poly stomach.

He also carries around a big bag like that of Daikokuten, who in the form of Sanmen Daikokuten I described earlier in the section on the Three Gods of Monetary Fortune. And since I did so, I will not profile his regular manifestation here. In fact it has a much bigger capacity than the one carried by Daikokuten. It is so crammed full that Hotei Osho has trouble even dragging it around.

Open it up and what do you find? All kinds of human voices call out. They raise a regular ruckus. Listen closely and you can hear individual voices badmouthing others, spitting out abuse or merely grumbling. In other words, this bag is chock full of the worst aspects of the human race.

But just when Hotei Osho cannot carry this bag any more and slumps down with a thud, and bows his head with a sigh, you catch the sound of still other voices coming out of the bag. These are bright, optimistic voices praising other people, urging diligence and calling urging their owners to get on with the job. So it is obvious, this magic bag also contains the good sides of people.

And in his right hand Hotei Osho also carries a fan, like the ones military leaders used to use as a symbol of their authority in old Japan. This is used to judge between good and evil. Although his head is smooth as polished metal, it is so sharp that he can quickly discern the truth in any situation.

Hotei Osho is also immensely fat. That is to show symbolically that he is capable of consuming anything. During a lifetime a person may be required to endure all kinds of things. At times he may have to take things from other people that he would prefer not to. He has to simply hide his true feelings, since any outburst may end up his own loss. The ability to shut up and ignore such unpleasant situations is extremely important in business. Self-control is a huge advantage. A short temper means big losses. So look before you leap, or shoot off your mouth. That is an incontestable, basic principle for the businessman who would be a success.

Hotei Osho uses his spiritual power, which is concentrated in his belly, to induce calm and a sense of proportion. And he employs his bag to get rid of insults and slander. Thus he is free to weigh dispassionately good and evil, truth and falsehood and reach a correct decision. If you are the type of person who tends to shoot from the lip, and talk all kinds of nonsense that alienates those around you, I urge you strongly to tune into the spiritual vibrations of Hotei Osho and mellow out.

Secret Method for Using Your Chances

One of Shogun Tokugawa Ieyasu's closest advisors was a Buddhist priest by the name of Tenkai. History tells us that he once advised Ieyasu, "Japanese should try to act just like the Seven Divinities of Good Luck." And he was right on that score. The personality characteristics represented by each of the seven are things that we all need.

Money is not everything in this world. But if you are interested in attaining good fortune with wealth, first try to cultivate thoroughly in your heart the distinctive characteristics of these seven deities. If you can create the proper conditions in your inner world, then good fortune will begin to appear of itself in the outer world.

Another point I would like to emphasize is that whether with the Seven Divinities of Good Luck, or the Three Gods of Monetary Fortune that I discussed earlier, it will not do to simply revere these deities. If you just beg, "Bestow on me good fortune! Please, oh please!" it is useless. You have got to get out there and work for it too. The gods will have none of it if you are not willing to do your part of the bargain.

Instead, cultivate your soul and four spirits, by trying to incorporate the virtues represented by the Seven Divinities of Good Luck and Three Gods of Good Monetary Fortune, which are really already present in you anyhow. Give them more leeway to have an impact and supplement your good side with power from the spiritual world. In this way seek to join hands with the gods on the path to success.

But the important thing is that you yourself strive and go looking for that old, elusive friend Good Fortune. Your efforts will be reflected in your heart and your attitude. And then the gods will look upon you approvingly and say, "Well, let's give this guy our full support."

The point is you need to get in the frame of mind where you think: "I'm not going to wait for the gods to move; my actions will set the divine world in motion."

I should also point out here that in recent years the number of people who understand how the divine world really operates and how to work with it has declined significantly. As a result, many of the gods have become saddened from lack of attention and if you do as I have suggested they will be more than willing to get behind you.

The Way You Pray is Important

Next I would like to explain the correct way to pray to the gods. As I mentioned before, never try to force the gods to do what you want. It is all-important to instead signal your willingness to help yourself and to adopt a positive attitude. Your prayer might be phrased like this: "I intend to do this much. So great gods, please stand by me and support me in my efforts."

Here, it is important to remember not just to call the god's name and say "Help me." Your prayer has to be offered in the right fashion. Christians, for example, do not just say, "Hey God!" They use specially formulated standard prayers like: "Our Father who art in Heaven, hallowed be Thy Name..."

The ritual prayers of Shinto, known as *norito*, very effectively employ set words to speak to the gods correctly. Examples of the proper form are included at the end of this book. But even if you are simply folding your hands to offer an informal, simple prayer, it still advisable to use set words. The key is to praise the god in question and to emphasize his particular characteristics.

For example, if you are praying to Bishamonten, you should say: *Oh you possessor of the mighty power to conquer evil, member of the band of Four Heavenly Gods....*

On the other hand if you are addressing Ebisu, you should say: Thou who has the enormous strength of will and perseverance to wait until you capture the giant sea bream...

These set words and phrases are a hundred times more powerful than just saying, *Please!* So is the help given by the deities who hear them! But think about it for a second and you will realize that this really makes sense. For instance, if a salesman comes to your front door unexpectedly and says, "Buy this product. I say buy it, so buy it!" What on earth are you going to think? Well, you know you are going to give him the cold shoulder.

But say the same salesman chats you up and says, "You really have a beautiful home here. And you dress with exquisite taste. You seem to know what you're doing when you buy things. Just take a look at this product I have here. It's a real bargain. And I'd say it matches your sense to a tee. I can guarantee that if you buy it, you'll never regret the move. I really would like to show you just how good it is. So won't you please give it a try."

When you have heard a good sales pitch like that, you are more likely to start saying to yourself. "We'll it doesn't look like I can miss by buying it. I'm getting a bargain to boot. I can tell this guy means what he says. So why not buy it?"

The gods think in the same way. If you bow your head reverently in prayer and pour your whole heart into real prayers, there is certain to be a reaction in the spirit world.

Furthermore, when you speak these set phrases, you will also reinforce your own feelings of piety and the specifically desired image. In this way, you can greatly strengthen your communication with the spirit world.

Of course, even while you are making sure that you have spirit power on your side, you cannot slough off when it comes to your own efforts. You also must develop a frame of mind in which you are concerned about the other guy as well as yourself.

And last but not least, when you pray to the divine world do not forget to couch your requests in terms like: *Should the divine world not want this for me, then please help me to rectify my course.* In other words: *Let Thy will not mine be done.*

What this really means is that you are ready in the end to leave your course of action and the outcome, in fact everything, up to the will of the gods.

Well, I have tried to explain how divine-inspired good fortune works from a number of different angles. But really the easiest and most important way to understand things is to give these principles a try yourself. If you experience in the flesh the kind of righteous profit willed by the gods and spiritual power, then you will know exactly what I mean.

There is no way you can understand the effects of divine grace and personal merit in terms of logic; you just have to experience them. I trust that if you do things properly your true good luck with money will increase by the day.

CHAPTER 3
Making Your Millions

Secrets for Acquiring Wealth From Around the World

Nationalities With the Midas Touch

Certain ethnic groups seem to have a special knack for making money. The Jews are number one without a doubt. They are followed by the Overseas Chinese and the Indians. The Japanese also are not at all bad in this regard.

It has been said that Jewish money controls the global economy and is especially powerful in the United States. The Jews are a remarkable people. Around 2,000 years ago they lost their homeland and were scattered across the face of the earth. But although they had to endure countless hardships including persecution as they wandered as exiles, they never gave up their faith in their god Yahweh nor their dream of restoring their nation. And they conscientiously passed these beliefs on to their children and grandchildren.

I can well understand how the Jews have accumulated such an immense amount of money, as to have attained virtual economic hegemony in the world. They also have tremendous power in the realm of politics as well. But the key to their success is not to be found in the *Protocols of Zion*, a work alleged to have been written by Jewish elders that details the "global strategy of the Jews," or any other book for that matter. The real root causes run much deeper, with influences to be found in actual conditions, history and the influences from the divine world.

There are actually four primary sources of Jewish power:

education, the divine world, blood ties and the historical environment.

First of all there is the fanatical Jewish devotion to education. From when they are small, Jewish children study the *Old Testament*. And the importance of God's covenant with Moses – what really amounts to his program for humankind – is pounded into their head. This type of education is so effective that sometimes it gives birth to geniuses like Albert Einstein.

Next, there is the role of the divine world. The Jews firmly believe in the promise that their god Yahweh made to them that they would be the Chosen People forever. This belief became the foundation of an amazing collective mindset among the entire Jewish people. This in turn led to the formation of a unique part of the divine world, so that "God" and his angels have indeed come down to earth to protect them.

Incidentally, in the divine world Yahweh is an immense golden dragon deity, a veritable powerhouse of authority and capabilities. He therefore has the ability to control untold amounts of money in the material world. So much money does he control, that he can determine the direction of nations and the entire world for that matter.

Then there are blood ties. The Jewish preoccupation with blood relations is incredible. So much so that it is difficult for we Japanese who have grown up in an isolated island country to imagine. Jews will gladly spend huge amounts of money without batting an eyelash in order to save a fellow Jew. It is really astounding. To them blood and spirit are one and the same. In other words, blood is nothing more than the spirit in concrete form.

Finally, there is the historical environment. Despite undergoing untold cases of persecution, the Jews were eventually able to reestablish their nation. The historical crucible in which they found themselves, toughened the Jews as individuals.

Education, the influence of the divine world, blood ties and the historical environment. These four factors worked to give the Jews certain advantages, while at the same time they were able to line up a strong bloc of support in the divine world. This in turn helped to bring them luck in the areas of money, power and abilities.

In many ways, the situations of the Jews and *hua-ch'iao*, or Overseas Chinese, are comparable. While living in exile in foreign lands, they too thickened their blood ties with members of their own ethnic group and developed enormous financial power.

Why the Japanese Have Succeeded

Next, let us consider why Japan today is an economic heavyweight that can boast the second largest GNP in the world. What factors have made this amazing success possible? No doubt, there are many contributing factors. Should I begin a real explanation, it would end up taking forever. Suffice it to say that the reasons can be summed up in the expression *Yamato damashii* or "the soul of Japan."

Yamato damashii is often used to describe the amazing physical courage that the Japanese have for example shown in war. But it means more than that as well. The Japanese people have a very highly developed talent for digesting various influences. That means that they are used to taking A and B and mixing them to create something new – namely C. At the same time, they are careful to preserve the old, even while seeking to cultivate the new.

A good example, especially relevant to the contents of this book, is Japanese religion. Throughout Japan's religious history,

everything from the ancient native religion of Shinto to Buddhism, Confucianism, Christianity, various kinds of religions have coexisted side by side without any hostility. And in the case of Buddhism, although this religion originated in distant India, it has flourished in Japan, the nation farthest east from its land of birth.

Japanese are basically not inclined to draw distinctions in their thinking, saying things like: "A is wrong, but B is right." Instead, they usually try to find a way to accommodate everything, saying: "A is good, and so is B."

This attitude is summed up in the expression: *Let's let bygones be bygones and forget about them as quickly as possible.* This is quite different from the message of fierce revenge advocated by Yahweh through the philosophy of: *An eye for an eye and a tooth for a tooth.*

Japan has its own spirit world. And it is only natural that Japanese should act in accordance with the dictates of that spirit world. By that I mean that nearly all the guardian spirits active here are our ancestors. And the tutelary gods too are pure "Born in Japan" deities. Consequently, if you expect to win Japan's spirit world over to your side so as to secure good luck with money, you should be prepared to take the collective consciousness of that spirit world into account.

Anyone who wants to call Japan his spiritual home should to the best of his ability seek to think and behave in a thoroughly Japanese way. If I had to give a name to that "Japanese way" I am speaking of, it would be none other than *Yamato damashii*. In other words, Japanese should never lose sight of the best they have to offer, whether it be in culture or whatever.

If you keep this point firmly in mind, when you attempt to get the spirit world to act in your behalf, you will find that you will be washed over by the special kind of power for good luck with money that is indigenous to the Japanese people and will thereby be able to ride a tremendous wave of luck to new accomplishments. As I will explain later, top Japanese businessmen and financial leaders have been able to concentrate this kind of uniquely Japanese good luck with money in their persons and as a result have achieved great success in their careers.

Ethnic Physical Differences

Oddly enough, it seems to me that ethnic groups that have good luck in money tend to have facial features that are similar in many ways. I hasten to add, however, that I personally have not had the opportunity to confirm this conclusion by observing in the flesh even a few hundred people who are of these ethnic groups. So I do not have any kind of statistics to back this assertion. But I do know that three conditions are required to give a person a spiritual aura:

a. Big bone structure

b. Large nose

c. Luster around the earlobes and bridge of the nose

By "big bone structure" I do not mean that the person necessarily has to be large. Many small individuals give the impression that they are big-boned. They are robust, healthy and on top of that extremely strong. That is why they are endowed with great strength of will and spiritual power.

Large noses are distinguished in their own right, and also strongly suggest inner power. Furthermore a large nose in the middle of a good face lends a sense of stability to the entire face. It indicates its owner will have good luck in the middle years of life and specifically with money. That is because of his looks the person can make the people he meets feel at their ease and cause others to think of him as trustworthy.

Luster around the earlobes and bridge of the nose really means that the entire facial skin has a certain attractive sheen to it. Such a rosy color is a sign that the person is healthy and indicates that he or she has possibilities for developing good luck, and is of a bright, open temperament characterized by sincerity.

This is admittedly a very rough characterization. But these features are generally found among nationalities with good luck power.

Problem Gods

Yahweh, the protective deity of the Jewish people, is a mighty god indeed. But he has one big flaw. He is extremely fond of strict commandments and rules.

The ten commandments handed down to Moses written in stone were dictated by this god. And one look at them reveals his personality. They are basically a collection of *Thou Shalt Nots.* They reveal Yahweh's concern for exhibiting his power and maintaining order. But their biggest flaw is that they refuse to make any leeway whatsoever for other religions.

To put it frankly, the Jewish tradition lacks the quality of love. Because there is no love, there is no forgiveness. And for that reason, it is easy for the spirit of revenge to take root.

Jesus Christ, who was of course born a Jew, was very perceptive about this flaw in the Jewish tradition. In so many words he emphasized that human beings cannot live by laws and commandments alone. They also require love. And love and god are really one and the same.

At first these commandments were no doubt created by Yahweh to help people live happily. But Jesus preached that love was more important than respecting mere rules. This was the very point that made Jesus a religious revolutionary. It was also what led him to say, *If someone slaps you on your right cheek, turn your left cheek to him also.*

Thus was born a new philosophy diametrically opposed to the old precept of *An eye for an eye, and a tooth for a tooth.* There was also the occasion on which Jesus berated the moneychangers and merchants flagrantly doing business in front of the Temple. The New Testament says that he even kicked their tables over with his foot. In other words, he was really taking a kick at the Golden Dragon God, who was the Jewish god of good luck. Furthermore, he violated Yahweh's commandment against work on the Sabbath by healing the sick and going into the fields.

This unorthodox attitude on the part of Jesus was one reason most of the Jews could not accept his message then and cannot accept it now. That point is highly significant.

You see, Yahweh "the Golden Dragon God" used his strict commandments and regulations to unite the Jewish people and to help them to make money. Jesus, on the other hand, declared that through love human beings could accumulate *treasures* in Heaven. Christ was talking about "true wealth" of the spiritual kind; Yahweh was talking about gold. Of course this is simplifying things far too much, but this is the general pattern.

Next we come to Mahomet, "the Prophet," who developed a marvelous synthesis in this regard. He urged that people employ love to gain spiritual "treasure," and then in turn rely on this "treasure" to win riches. Mahomet was spiritually extremely shrewd in the way he juxtaposed these two concepts of love and the power of the Dragon God.

And I might also note in this regard that the incredible tolerance and eclecticism so evident in Japan's spiritual world means that its people can recognize both the Golden Dragon God and Christianity's emphasis on love as forms of wealth without the slightest bit of contradiction or conflict.

Well, in a few short paragraphs I have attempted to sketch how spiritual power operates differently among various ethnic groups and thereby influences luck with money. The important thing is not to become fixated on only one form of fortune. Better to adopt a more broadminded approach. That I suppose is quintessentially the Japanese way of thinking. If you think only in terms of "this is the only way" or "this must be," then you are certain to lose many lucky opportunities, since luck is something that is always undergoing change.

I should also point out that there are dozens of dragon deities that can effect luck with money and they come in all kinds of varieties: blue, white, red, yellow, silver and wood. If you are interested, I go into a much more detailed explanation of these dragons in *The Divine World*.

The Money Philosophy and Past Lives of Leading Japanese Businessmen

Spiritual Vibrations From the Top
Reach Every Corner of a Firm

As I think anyone with experience in the field will attest, it is not that easy to run a firm and continue to boost profits.

There are all kinds of problems to be considered: product

management and development, personnel matters, social change, capital acquisition, tax policy, cash flow and so on.

A good manager has to have highly attuned antenna to be able to react properly in all these areas. He also constantly is aware that if he makes the wrong decisions, the company is likely to go under, thereby throwing the lives of its employees and their families into chaos. At the very least, he has to realize that his own thinking and corporate ideals will affect the fate of more individuals than just himself.

On the other hand, should a manager be blessed with good monetary fortune, his firm will be able to develop smoothly and as a result he can raise the salaries of his employees. The key to the monetary fortune of the employees of most companies really lies in the hands of its managers. That makes their responsibility all the more weighty.

In addition, even if a manager personally has good fortune, that does not necessarily mean that he will be able to extend it to the level of his company. At the very least, the power of that good fortune alone will not be enough to do the trick. Individuals who have made it to the top of the corporate ladder or who have founded and built up a great firm from scratch exude a personal magnetism that draws others to them. This is something quite different from good fortune; it is something like natural virtue.

Good managers also almost inevitably take good care of their people. As one famous soldier once put it: *My men are my walls; my men are my citadel.* The same holds true for a company. The company employee is the key. The ability of the employees recruited and the degree to which their full potential is tapped will determine the collective power of a given company. So it is the job of the manager to try to retain his best people.

152

Put another way, that means that it is important for a company to develop corporate ideals that will win the loyalty of the best people. A company is really just a collection of people, things and money. Things are made by it to win the attention of other people and thereby make money. Success depends on whether or not operations are performed skillfully. A manager who is no good at figures will ultimately not be able to lead his employees properly nor take full advantage of the human resources at his disposal.

And the ideal and *personality* of a firm are greatly influenced by the spiritual level of its top man and the spiritual vibrations he gives off. The thinking of this top man and how he decides to go about seeking profit in the world are very important considerations. It would be no exaggeration to say that to a considerable extent the ideals of the president or whoever else is really in charge of a company permeate the entire firm.

In fact, although they remain invisible, the spiritual vibes given off by this top man affect the sales force, the workers in the factory and even the women at the reception desk. That is to say, they go far in determining the firm's corporate identity (CI), a factor we hear much of these days in relation to corporate strategy.

Strange as it may seem, there are also many cases where the president of a company will be thinking about a certain section at a certain plant and just then there will be a knock on his door. And, lo and behold, his caller turns out to be the manager of that very section. This is evidence that the spiritual vibrations given off by the president have had an effect on that section chief.

Managers Who Seize Their Chances

As I explained in Chapter 1, it is good to have the right kind of desire, a bit of egoism and big dreams. It is definitely bad however to become too headstrong and abnormally unbending. Such a person's mental vision becomes clouded over and his genius becomes dulled. If these traits are displayed only at the personal level, then they will only result in loss and failure for that individual. But that is not true when such a person holds a position of authority in a company or other organization.

A manager who has to judge subtle economic trends and then make the right decisions on corporate strategy is dealing in a different dimension from personal likes and dislikes. To know how to advance boldly when chances present themselves and how to retreat adroitly and with no regrets when the tide is running against you. Such skills are the mark of a great corporate leader. Consequently, a manager needs to sharpen his wits each day when it comes to seizing chances that might come his way. It is all-important to know when is the right time for moving or holding ground.

The deity who controls the instinctual understanding of *time* is Ko-no-hana-sakuya-hime-no-kami, the goddess of Mt. Fuji. Ko-no-hana is a name used in ancient times for the cherry blossom. As you no doubt are aware, the cherry blossom blooms quickly and then falls from its bough only a few short days later. Without a tinge of regret, it gives itself to the spring breezes. The point here is that if you want to develop your skills for judging the moment and grasping opportunity, then it is important to take as your model the spirit of the cherry blossom, which shows a combination of resoluteness and a willingness to sacrifice the ego. It blooms or falls with equal equanimity.

154

I am sure the difference between successful and unsuccessful managers is to be found precisely here. Recently, for example, we have seen several venture businesses achieve great success by being able to seize the moment and take advantage of opportunities they discerned. Of course, quite a few venture business go bankrupt after enjoying a fleeting moment of glory. But in most of those cases, their president has been the hard-working, hard-headed, "my way" type, who is inclined to leap before he looks.

The situation is usually quite different at the venture businesses that make it. The bosses of these firms also tend to appear to be strong-willed, but actually they are usually willing to listen to the opinions of others. It is clear that venture businesses that achieve high growth solely on the basis of the personal good fortune of their owners or presidents are destined for a fall in the long run. It is because they become infatuated with their own skill and become too fixated on them.

There are some big companies around today that started as the equivalent of today's venture businesses. So we should view a given venture business as perhaps the "second Sony" or "second Honda." You could even say that the men who founded the houses that developed into today's *zaibatsu* - huge economic groups like Mitsubishi or Sumitomo - were richly endowed with the venture business mentality and spirit. The reason why these various firms could grow from small "venture businesses" into world-dominating corporate goliaths is that the men at the top did not become enamored of their own talents, but always displayed a willingness to listen to the opinions of others.

It is especially difficult to make the transition from a small business to a middle-size business, or from a middle-size business to a large business. It often boils down to whether the top man is willing to develop managers who are his equals in talent. But unless people are put in charge of the sales, financial, labor, product development, and advertising sides of the business, who are blessed with their own good fortune, then it will be very difficult for a company to make the leap up to the next stage. Moreover, if a corporate leader refuses to purge himself of pride and obstinacy and adopt an open attitude towards the advice of others, then he is likely to miss seeing any possible pitfalls. And therefore Ko-no-hana-sakuya-hime-no-kami, the deity of the timely moment, will not smile on him.

The Effects of Past Lives

I have already described the connections between our present lives and past lives. You should be aware, however, consciousness of past lives submerged in his subconscious will greatly color the corporate ideals a president distills in a company and its other characteristics.

Perfect examples, would be the late Konosuke Matsushita, founder of the mammoth Matsushita group of electrical and electronic product companies, Toshio Doko, who before his death was honorary chairman of the Keidanren and dean of Japan's business community, Soichiro Honda, founder of Honda Motor Corporation, and Akio Morita of Sony. We might also include the late Kenji Osano, considered by many as one of the most influential postwar businessmen with special connections with the political world.

I should hasten to add that I have never had the honor of meeting any of these gentlemen, and I am not well versed in their personal corporate theory and philosophy. I am merely speaking from my experience as a spiritualist researcher who has had contact with the worlds of the spirits and has witnessed the influence of their past lives on them.

"If you haven't even met these individuals, how can you possibly judge the effects of their past lives?" The many doubters among the readers of this book would be justified in asking that question. But I guarantee you that it is not an impossibility if you can concentrate supernatural powers. I will not go into details here. But suffice it to say that even if the individual is not present, it is possible to see such a person's past lives or his guardian spirits.

Of course, it is more reliable to meet the person directly, since otherwise you have to observe things from a more remote distance, which demands the very greatest powers of concentration.

As for why I am discussing the previous lives of these businessmen here, it is because factors related to money and luck with finance that affect the fate of a company or the nation as a whole inevitably are tied to the influence of the spirit world. Actually, smaller amounts of money are also affected by the attitudes of the spirits.

"Why is that guy so good at making money?" Many people no doubt have such a sense of admiration for the kind of people I am talking about. And these individuals no doubt do have a real knack for keeping good monetary fortune around them for a long period of time. But at the same time, you should remember that sometimes the consciousness lurking below the surface that reminds an individual that he did not make it in his past life causes him to put out that much more to succeed this time around. Sometimes it seems that it is not the drive to make money, but something beyond that that makes a businessman.

Usually people whose credo is *making money is the only reason for being alive* do not end up heading companies with hundreds or thousands of employees. Or even if they do, the company usually goes under after only one generation. Really making money should be considered only a means to an end. The ultimate goals of a businessman should be to bring happiness to others, contribute to society and work for the continued development of the company and the welfare of its employees. The businessman who thinks like that will make the divine world happy and win its help and protection.

Konosuke Matsushita

The late Konosuke Matsushita (1894-1989), founder of the Matsushita electric products empire, was one of the most famous entrepreneurs in the world and his rags-to-riches story has served as inspiration to countless businessmen. However, few realize that in a previous life he was none other than the founder of the Ming Dynasty (1368-1644), Emperor T'ai Tsu ("Great Progenitor"), whose original name was Chu Yuan-chang. He was born into a poor peasant family but eventually rose to the pinnacle of society as the "Son of Heaven," just as Emperor Kao Tsu (Liu Pang), founder of the Han Dynasty, had before him. In the spring of his seventeenth year, Yuan-chang lost his parents and all his brothers to disease.

Now an orphan, for a time he underwent rigorous spiritual training as a novice Buddhist monk. Then he became a soldier, where he made his mark and rose to the rank of general.

Yuan-chang was finally able to expel the Mongols and found the Ming (meaning "bright") Dynasty in 1368 when he was 40. Because the era name then was called Hung-wu, he became known as the Hung-wu ("Vast Military Power") Emperor (this name was derived from a year period name) and ruled the vast Chinese empire under that title. The new emperor proved as adept at politics as he had in military affairs, revitalizing the villages, providing education for the peasants and conducting accurate population surveys, among other things. On the other hand, Hung-wu was paranoid about opposition and mercilessly exterminated perhaps 30,000 "enemies."

It was true though that any man who would rule the vast land of China had to display iron authority. So to a certain degree he no doubt could not avoid being ruthless. In any event, Hung-wu died in 1398 at age 71.

All of this happened six centuries ago. Eventually, the spirit of Chu Yuan-chang, the man who had united China under the Ming, was reborn as Konosuke Matsushita. In fact the same spirit entered this world again as Matsushita almost exactly 500 years after the death of Chu.

As most people know, Matsushita was born into a poor family. Actually, at the time he was born in 1894 nearly all Japanese were poor. But in Matsushita's case, not only was he poor, his body was also frail. At nine Matsushita went to work as an apprentice. Later he became a factory worker at an electric light company in Osaka. While there he contrived a double-outlet electric socket and then at the tender young age of 37 left to start up his own company. The breakup of the *zaibatsu* during the Occupation caused him considerable problems, but when the electrical appliance boom began in the late 1950s, he was ready and thereafter enjoyed considerable success. In fact, Matsushita proceeded to build the world's largest electronics and electrical appliance empire. Obviously there are similarities between Konosuke Matsushita, who although born into poverty founded Japan's top home electrical appliance firm, and Chu Yuan-chang, a Chinese poor boy who made himself master of the Middle Kingdom. Looking at their respective portraits, you can see certain similarities in their faces.

Matsushita was long known as *the God of Management.* But when I looked into his affairs in the spirit world not too long before his death in 1990, I found that he had actually achieved only about 70% of what he had originally set out to do and that the remaining 30% was a source of some vexation to him.

I do not really want to get into Matsushita's private life, but when he was around 17 he had an experience that made him consider deeply the meaning of life and set high ambitions for himself. Because of the amazing determination that he showed, he attracted a large host of protective deities and they backed him up completely thereafter.

In fact, Matsushita eventually built up an army of guardian spirits between 2,300 and 2,500 strong, roughly half of whom are Chinese. The karmic connection between Matsushita and Emperor Hung-wu is thus reflected in the makeup of his corps of protectors. Incidentally, and I do not mean this in a bad sense, Matsushita appraised others in a very cold, detached manner.

Sometimes that attitude appeared to be even calculating and hard-headed. But this cool, detached way of thinking seems to have helped Matsushita build his empire, so it probably was a plus in the end.

Atonement for Past Lives

Chu Yuan-chang certainly lived a righteous life, and so did Matsushita. Proof of that was the fact that within the grounds of the home office of the Matsushita organization he established a shrine

to worship the "fountainhead" of the universe. Matsushita also at one time served as chairman of a major group of Ise Shrine worshippers and a group representing Shinto shrines all over Japan.

In this fashion, the faith Chu Yuan-chang developed as a monk flowered in a different age. The fact that in spiritual matters Matsushita showed very eclectic sensibilities and was willing to accept appropriate additions from any source was also a perfect reflection of the spirit of *Yamato damashii* I explained earlier.

In order to maintain his power, Chu Yuan-chang ordered many men killed. But these evil deeds could not be atoned for completely through ascetic self-training in the spirit world after he died. So some of that bad karmic influence remained after he was reborn as Matsushita.

Luckily for Matsushita, as it turned out over the long run, during his youth he suffered terribly from poverty, illness and a poor education. And of course, money, health and a good education are normally the three most important ingredients of success in this world. But his trials and tribulations served to lighten the burden carried over from a previous existence that had been placed on Matsushita's shoulders as a child.

No matter how much a man might have faith in the gods, how many good works he might do or contributions make, the deities cannot completely wipe the slate clean for the record of his past lives. The reason for that is that the person himself must reap the harvest of the karmic seeds that he has sowed. Even the gods themselves cannot alter the general principle of all creation that good brings good and evil brings evil. After all it is a principle established by the gods themselves.

However, they do have the ability to reduce the debt so to speak through their overwhelming compassion. And sufferings of the individual also help to lessen the debt. Here it is important to point out that suffering when a person is young is much more effective in this regard than after he is elderly. Suffering also serves as an important stimulus to further human growth. The more hardships a person endures when he is small, the more the gods will love him. Matsushita was able to overcome the hardships of his youth in remarkable fashion. Thereafter, he was a man of the highest ambitions who always oriented his life towards the future. That is the reason why he was able to garner so much support among the spirits.

Also, although of course I never heard this from Mr. Matsushita directly, I am convinced that at least seven times during his lifetime he wanted so badly to escape the bitter situation he was facing that he felt like dying. Two of these experiences were especially difficult. On those occasions, the Ryuju Bodhisattva came to the rescue and instilled him with the courage he needed. Incidentally, the reason why Matsushita achieved such a deep understanding of business and human nature was that this same bodhisattva, who acted something like a representative of his guardian spirits, provided him with backup power.

As I explained earlier, Matsushita had an army of guardian spirits numbering more than 2,000. And this legion of spiritual troopers helped Matsushita spread his personal philosophy, sometimes referred to as *Matsushitaism,* among every last one of his tens of thousands of employees. It worked like this. If Matsushita started thinking, "I wonder if the people in that division have really got it yet?" the spirits would be affected by this idea and rush to that particular division and exert their special guardian spirit power to make sure that the workers had indeed got the message. Conversely, the clear affection of his workers for Matsushita also served to attract the spirits.

The activation of guardian spirit power and its influence on us are things which we experience frequently in our daily lives. For example, isn't it true that lovers or married couples have certain psychic ties when they are bonded by true mutual respect and affection? They will think something like, "I wonder what he's doing at this very moment?" And it will suddenly seem like that person is there right beside her.

Such sensations are caused by the psychic vibrations given off by the main spirits and the guardian spirits involved. In Matsushita's case, because of the huge number of guardian spirits arrayed behind him, this spirit power reached staggering proportions.

Well, I am sure you will agree that with all the spiritual interaction going on here the importance of interaction among employees and senior managers in our *real* world cannot be overemphasized. A CEO who does not command the respect and devotion of his workers spiritually speaking has already lost his qualifications to lead the corporation.

Be warned, however, that there are also some senior managers who have reached the top solely on the basis of personal charisma and who manipulate and deceive others solely in order to make money. Employees who become enamored with such a boss are truly tragic and pathetic. The reason is that they will soon fall under the influence of the evil spirits that hover around such a deceitful manager.

Kenji Osano

To be honest, there was a time when I hardly knew anything at all about Kenji Osano, the wheeler dealer who made so many headlines back when Kakuei Tanaka was prime minister. Of course,

I also have never met the man nor had any conversation with him. All I knew was what I read in the newspapers or heard on the TV news, namely that he was a "bosom buddy" of Tanaka.

Nevertheless, after his death back in 1986 the weekly magazines were filled with articles saying things like his estate was worth trillions of yen and that he had around 20,000 employees. Even now I can recall how surprised I was at that time to hear that he had that kind of money and influence. He was in fact perhaps the richest or second richest man in Japan at that time and within the very top echelons of the ranks of the wealthiest people in the entire world.

It was really bizarre that the name of such a super-rich and powerful individual should only have been brought up by the mass media at the time of the Lockheed Scandal trials. That was ample evidence of just how skilled Osano had been at operating in the shadows. Anyhow, all of this got me interested in the question of Osano's previous lives. Not that I hoped to confront him with the knowledge or gain any advantage from it, mind you.

Well anyhow, my investigations showed that in his past life Osano was Saito Dosan. Actually, it would be more correct to say that Saito's spirit was transferred directly into the body of Osano.

Saito Dosan was born in 1494, during the Muromachi Period. The son of a tradesman in Yamazaki in the province of Mino near Kyoto, Dosan won the nickname mamushi Dosan or "snake Dosan" because of his Machiavellian wiles. He started his career as a cooking oil salesman, but soon moved on to bigger things. Japan at that time was wracked by brutal civil wars and so chaotic had the situation become that many vassals, even some non-samurai, took advantage of the disorder to displace their hereditary overlords. The period thus gave birth to the phenomenon of *gekokujo* or "the low oppressing the high." In other words, "dog eat dog" was the prevailing moral code of the day.

Dosan was a perfect illustration of this trend. He enjoyed rapid advancement under his local lord, until he decided to turn on him and steal his castle. His sly stratagems won him that nickname *mamushi Dosan*. And he preferred them to brute force. That was shown in the way in which he gradually usurped the authority of the family who had done so much for him, and then simply installed himself as the new lord. To use wiles instead of weapons was clearly Dosan's wont.

However, Dosan had a major weakness Although he had seized the strategic Inabayama Castle and brought all of Mino under his sway, he did not have an appropriate heir. Until the very end, he tried a variety of stratagems to survive, such as marrying his daughter Nohime to the up-and-coming warlord Oda Nobunaga, but ironically he was killed in battle by the forces of "his own son" Yoshitatsu. This boy had in him blood of the previous lord who had been driven out of Mino.

So in a sense, even though Dosan had been able to win enormous riches, the last years of his life were hell on earth. He was 63 when he died in 1565.

As for Kenji Osano, when he was 18 or 19, he had terrible troubles that nearly killed him. It was at that time that the spirit of Saito Dosan replaced the original spirit he had been born with. So he must have undergone a complete transformation inside at this time.

"What, are you telling me that this guy's own spirit just disappeared some place and another man's spirit came walking in instead. Is such a thing really possible?"

No doubt many of my readers are asking just this question. As hard as it may be to believe, it is absolutely true.

In certain cases where a person suffers so much that he is close to death, he comes out of the experience appearing to be a totally different individual inside. This changing of personalities is exactly that; a new spirit moves in and sets up shop in place of the previous resident. A new spirit can also take over if a person loses consciousness because of high fever or shock. When low-level evil spirits do the possessing, we have the phenomenon known as "fox possession." But when a spirit overflowing with a sense of mission is involved as in the case of Osano, you get an exhibition of enormous spirit power.

Dosan first made a fortune as a wholesaler of oil. And interestingly enough, it is alleged that in the immediate postwar period when gas was still rationed, Osano established his own company to sell petroleum on the black market and made an enormous amount of money through it. The aptitude he showed for selling oil was clearly a "Dosan-style skill."

Black Dragon Protection

Later Osano made the acquaintance of the future prime minister Kakuei Tanaka, although at that time he was still only a dietman representing a rural district of Niigata Prefecture. Osano and Tanaka apparently hit it off right away and thereafter the pair progressed in tandem to the pinnacles respectively of the business and political worlds. Osano's reputation as a "political businessman" was earned because of the way he insinuated himself into the good graces of influential politicians. This was much like the way the merchant Dosan had initially won favor with his lord in what is now Gifu Prefecture. Osano clearly shared Dosan's style of doing things.

Dosan started off with just the shirt on his back, but eventually

rose to be a lord in his own right. Later generations have regarded Dosan with awe as a master strategist. And after his death, he underwent quite rigorous training in the spirit world. It also appears that Osano was distantly related to Dosan on his mother's side, so that was probably why the latter chose to inhabit his physical form to come back to the world in this present age.

Osano's original spirit had a fragile side to it and his original intelligence was no match for Dosan's. But once the spirits had changed places, Osano suddenly became sharp as a sword's edge and his personality became steadfast. Thereafter, he started establishing political connections left and right and piling up wealth.

Incidentally, the *new Osano* also had the assistance of two black dragon gods who had been protecting Dosan. Other supporters included a white snake and two Inari foxes. And a gold dragon god also sometimes put in an appearance as well. Black dragon gods, by the way, are manifestations of the gods O-kuni-nushi-no-mikoto and Sho-myo-hiko-no-mikoto and are the most powerful of all the dragon gods. They usually appear when the country is in disorder and bestow on those they decide to favor great leadership skills and enormous good luck in financial dealings and politics.

We can only speculate as to what sense of mission Osano had towards modern day Japan that would have caused Dosan's spirit to occupy his body. And we'll have to leave it to future generations to judge his contributions. Here in all innocence I simply want to show how the influence of the spirit world has affected his career.

Just let me add that black dragons and gold dragons are only attracted to great people who have a major effect on the course of history. Also, you might like to know that in his previous life Saito Dosan had also enjoyed much glory. He had been a member of the

Abbas clan and a general leading its armies that overthrew the Early Umaya (661-750) dynasty of caliphs who controlled much of the Middle East.

As I noted before, to be completely accurate we should not say that Kenji Osano was the reincarnation of Saito Dosan, rather his departed soul took control of Osano's body. If you can understand what is going on here, then you can see how such relationships can be even stronger than the normal ties between present and previous lives.

When he was alive Osano certainly did not go around saying, "I am Dosan Saito." But there can be no doubt that subliminally Dosan-like ideas were exerting an extremely strong force, which affected the way he acted and provided spirit-power backup for his efforts. Osano's features, the look in his eyes, his wiliness, the way he carried himself when walking....they were the spitting image of Dosan and his ways from 400 years before.

Toshio Doko

Toshio Doko was the acknowledged dean of the Japanese business community before his death in 1988. He was also well known as a devout believer in the power of the Lotus Sutra. There are numerous anecdotes about him, many no doubt apocryphal. But they generally attribute to him the following characteristics:

1. extreme simplicity in his lifestyle, 2. strict rules in this lifestyle, 3. tough even when he was over 80, 4. always tried to get the most out of life, but gave most of his personal fortune to educational activities.

The general impression of Doko was that his daily lifestyle resembled that of a Buddhist priest undergoing spiritual austerities.

He eschewed luxury and did not have any strong desires for material possessions. And he worked hard every single day. In fact he worked so hard that he made the spirits want to yell out encouragement like. "Hang in there!" or "You're doing sensational." Whether it was his honesty, his sense of old-fashioned stick-to-itness, or his vitality, what it was exactly is hard to say, but Doko had an enormous personal magnetism.

I had an intuition that Doko must have had some amazing past life and a little investigation proved me right. In fact, he had been none other than the Heian Period (794-1185) aristocrat Fujiwara Michitsuna. For much of that period the Fujiwara were the most prominent family in the realm and history books are replete with the names of illustrious Fujiwara family members. But Michitsuna did not win any great notice, with the exception of having his name mentioned in the literary work *Kagero Nikki* or *Gossamer Diary*.

It is recorded in the history books that Michitsuna (955-1020) made steady progress up the ladder of officialdom during the mid years of the Heian Period. But that is about all, besides the information that he became a priest after falling ill and then died a few days later. He was 65.

Michitsuna lived an average life within close proximity to the corridors of power. I can almost conjure up the image of Michitsuna as an official, slaving away at his work without complaint. It should not seem odd that sometimes his image and that of Doko overlap.

But my explanation would be insufficient if I did not describe that the ultimate source of spiritual power for both men was Nichirenism, in other words unwavering devotion to the Lotus Sutra. Michitsuna lived prior to Nichiren, so there is no reason why he should have shared the same beliefs as Doko. But the fact that he should have entered the religious life shortly before his death captured my attention. In other words, up until that time he had been a Buddhist layman. That in turn made me think of Doko who did everything he could to spread the message of the Lotus Sutra even while he performed wonders as a modern businessman.

Doko was sometimes referred to as *a living Nichiren*, and I believe that characterization was actually quite accurate. What I mean by that statement is that during the course of every day the departed soul of Saint Nichiren would come down to encourage Doko in his efforts on the job. He would also make his presence known in the mornings when Doko did his devotional chanting of the powerful expression Namu Myoho Renge Kyo, "Praise be the Holy Lotus Sutra." Then too when Doko was perplexed by questions concerning business or life, Nichiren would whisper to his innermost being what was the correct path to follow.

Mid-life Crises

Doko was born in 1896, but when he was in his 80s he was still much younger physically and mentally than his contemporaries. Most men reach their peak in those regards when they are in their 20s and 30s. And that is also the period of life in which most geniuses do their greatest work.

But in the case of Doko, there was no loss of vitality, and in fact until right up to his death he continued to show the enthusiasm for his work of a man in his 20s. One of the stories most often told about Doko is that when he was an executive at Ishikawajima-Harima Heavy Industries Co. he prided himself on his record of never having missed a day's work or never having been late to the office over a 40-year span. This record is proof of his strong

resolution, stamina and enviable stick-to-itness.

Although it might be said that Doko was blessed by Heaven with good health, it also must be admitted that most of Doko's good fortune was due to his own tremendous efforts. Every day after he finished his chanting to the Lotus Sutra, Doko began a new day. When considered as part of his entire 24-hour day, the time Doko spent on his chanting and similar activities might not have seemed to have amounted to much, but the fact that Doko prayed every single day without fail and with his whole heart and soul is evidence of his greatness. Even if someone had wanted to imitate him in order to follow in his path of success, it would not have been such a simple thing to do.

Earlier in this book, I promised that if you worked like the devil for a mere three months, and if you lived your life according to strict standards for three years, you would be sure to give full expression to your talents and thus be able to make it in the world and get wealthy. But just look at Doko – no three months for him. He worked all out every day as a businessman and was still working that way when he died in his 90s. You have to really make an effort like that if you expect to have the kind of good fortune that will change the course of Japan like he did.

But it would be a grave misconception to believe that Doko's success was all clear sailing. It is clear that just like the rest of us Doko had his problems and things that worried him. (Actually, his problems were of a different scale from ours.)

I believe that the period between when he was 54 and 58 was especially rough for Doko. I do not know if he was troubled inside, but he certainly had many difficulties to overcome. And the experiences of that period caused a major change inside him – a kind of personal waking up, so that he came to view things differently. And it was just about then that the departed soul of Saint Nichiren began to pay his visits once a day to Doko to lend him support.

It may seem a bit impertinent for me to say this, but I would like to try to recreate the kind of language I believe Saint Nichiren used when talking to Doko. He spoke of things Doko was no doubt well aware of.

Don't waver the slightest in your convictions. And keep doing your best till the day you die.

I truly believe that this is the kind of language that Nichiren used when speaking with Doko and encouraging him each day to make further spiritual and moral progress. All of us need to work unceasingly to achieve the same kind of progress in our quest for a true synthesis of the human and the divine.

Faith in the Lotus Sutra

The number of brain cells we can operate with is decided at birth. The key thereafter to stimulating mental activity is to try to attain the greatest possible coordination among these brain cells. Brains of people who are utilizing their heads for all they are worth are covered with deep wrinkles. That is an indication that collectively the cells are operating for all they are worth.

I am not an expert on the brain, so I am unfamiliar with the details of its remarkable mechanisms. But I can tell you this much, you will not find any presidents of large companies whose brains are operating at a sluggish pace. They are also usually in top shape for their age. Konosuke Matsushita, for example, remarked once that he expected to live until he was 120. Doko was still in the pink well into his 80s.

Why should it be that men like this who have such great responsibilities and are always under great pressure should as a rule enjoy such good health. The main reason is the power of their faith and the strength of their convictions. In Doko's particular case, it was of course the power of his faith in the Lotus Sutra. It was the ultimate source of his good health and all the rest of his fine qualities. And since all of his thinking was focused on living a life of righteousness, he was able to rally the support of the entire spirit world behind him.

No doubt the spiritual waves emitted by the spiritual world combine with the mental concentration of a person to invigorate the cells throughout his body, especially in the brain, and provide even more power. It seems that tens of thousands of cells die in the brain of an adult every single day. But if you can activate a greater number, all things considered, you should be able through the power of your faith, your convictions and concentration, and your inquiring mind and love of the truth to generate spiritual waves and increase their effectiveness.

What I am saying is that although the degeneration of the body and the mind due to the natural phenomenon of aging may appear inevitable, if your faith is strong enough you can actually reverse the process to an extent and become younger! This is nothing less than a miracle, in which the impossible becomes possible.

Anyhow, what effects did his unceasing labors have on Doko's position with the spiritual world; in other words around what tentative rank did he have not too long before his death when he was about to enter the spirit world? It may have been a little disrespectful of me, but l decided to take a peek at that time, using my powers of clairvoyance.

Through my contacts with the spirits I learned that he was ranked in the Second Heavenly Kingdom, and very close to the entrance to the First Heavenly Kingdom at that. Just on the very verge of entering the First Heavenly Kingdom in fact. It seems that all he needed to do to make the final push was to supplement his vast reservoir of faith with a little bit of love.

That was where he stood as of October 28, 1986. But it should be understood that the Second Heavenly Kingdom where he was ranked at that time is not a place that just anyone can go to. It is very high in the overall scheme of the spiritual world. So the rest of us mere mortals had reason to be very envious of Mr. Doko. But since anything is possible if we do our very, very best we should not rule out the possibility that we too could reach such ethereal heights some day. Instead we should seek to learn lessons from Doko about the value of hard work.

Doko's Aid to Education

One great point of similarity between Toshio Doko and his spirit in an earlier life, Fujiwara Michitsuna, was the importance they placed on education. Doko gave much of his private wealth to the Tachibana Academy for Women, where his own mother had served as principal. This institution bases its teaching on the principles and the teachings of the Nichiren sect. All of Doko's tangible assets and a good part of his income went to help operate this school.

That alone would certainly qualify Doko as a man with a burning zeal for education. But we also need to bear in mind his karmic ties to Fujiwara Michitsuna, whose mother wrote *The Gossamer Diary*. She was one of the many mistresses of Fujiwara Kaneiye, who at that time held the rank of Kampaku, or virtual dictator of the government. Michitsuna, born in 955, was the result of their union.

However, after his birth Kaneiye's ardor for Michitsuna's mother faded, and the children of his principal wife, Toki-hime, including the third son, Michizane – one of the most famous figures in all Japanese history – rose rapidly in the world. All these circumstances caused great suffering for Michitsuna's mother and she wrote about her feelings in subtle but elegant fashion in *The Gossamer Diary*.

So we have the connection between this literary masterpiece from the brush of Michitsuna's mother and the Tachibana school, where Doko's mother served as principal. Very interesting and persuasive parallels between past and present lives, I might say.

Anyhow, I should not forget to point out that at peak times Doko's gang of guardian spirits numbered somewhere around 7,000. When he would go out in his garden to do a bit of hoeing, at least 100 would be on watch around him. Doko was something like a feudal lord of old, what with his 7,000 personal spiritual attendants. Furthermore, Doko's famous work on behalf of restructuring the Japanese economy and otherwise helping it out was given a boost by another protective deity, a white dragon god.

White dragons are the essence of water coalesced into tangible form. Their role is not only to make sure that those they protect can gather enormous sums of capital; they also help move the economy in general. The Sumiyoshi Taisha Shrine in Kansai, for example, is dedicated to a white dragon, which exerts great power from there.

Incidentally, white dragons which have had their wings clipped (so to speak) so that they are earth-bound are referred to as white snake gods. These are the same white snake gods who protected Konosuke Matsushita and brought him such stupendous good fortune. Unfortunately, however, the white snake gods do not have the same scale of power as the white dragon gods. But sometimes a person has to start from nothing, and they have a very big role to play in such cases.

That was exactly what happened with Matsushita. It was only when he reached age 72 that Matsushita also got some white dragon gods and other powerhouses of the spiritual world to be his protectors. This was a reward no doubt for the enormous contributions he had made to the welfare of Japan about that time.

Akio Morita

Sony has become a household name around the world. One of its two co-founders, Masaru Ibuka, has already more or less retired, although he still holds the title of Honorary Chairman. The other, Akio Morita, is still going strong and it is he who holds the real power in the firm. And since Morita was born in 1921, he has several good working years left in him and his influence has probably only just begun to be felt. For that reason I cannot really get too much into details here about Morita's former lives, considering Sony's position in Japan and the world. But I will give you the reader just a bit of information for your own reference.

Believe it or not Morita's earlier life was at the time of the American Revolution two centuries ago, when he served as a commodore in the American forces fighting the British.

Unfortunately, I could not locate the name of anybody fitting that description in the biographical dictionaries I have. But according to the little bit of information I have, I suspect he was the traditional founder of the American navy and its leader during the early years – John Paul Jones. If you remember, Jones was the man who challenged the Royal Navy, "Ruler of the Seven Seas." He was a brave fellow who prided himself on his all-around versatility.

To tell you the truth, I have no idea what the connection is between audio equipment and the navy. But since the master inventor Ibuka was in his former life a British aristocrat, there seems to be some strange kind of Anglo-American connection at work here. Since I am not well-versed concerning either Ibuka or Morita, I will not venture any farther than to tell you that.

However, back 200 years ago America was merely a collection of colonies under the control of Great Britain, which was then the most powerful nation on earth. When the 1~ colonies declared their independence, they were taking 011 not only their motherland, but also an empire with the strongest military and navy on earth.

True a national battle for independence and the struggle to help your company get ahead are two very different things. But they both represent leaps into the dark – on one hand in America's struggle for independence and opening up of a new land, and on the other hand revolutionary breakthroughs in audio-visual equipment. But I think we can trace Morita's famous fierce resoluteness to subliminal influences from his subconscious harkening back to this previous life of revolutionary action. Furthermore, I believe we can expect to see a lot more interesting activity on the part of Morita.

Soichiro Honda

Another maverick of Japan's business world is motorcycle and automobile manufacturer Soichiro Honda. In fact, he is the best example of a businessman who has benefited from the influence of his past lives. Let me again hasten to add, I have never met Honda nor worked with him or his company in any capacity. But I do know for sure that his scale and manner of thinking are big enough to transcend national boundaries.

Actually, this boldness of vision and action come naturally to Honda, considering that in his past life he was Captain James Cook.

Cook (1728-79) was born into a poor British peasant family on the eve of the Industrial Revolution. When he was 27 he entered the Royal Navy, which proved a fateful decision. Because of his towering genius for navigation, he was ordered to undertake his great voyages of exploration.

He more than fulfilled the expectations placed in him and in his three great voyages he discovered many, many islands. During the second of these journeys, he completed the first successful circumnavigation of Antarctica and the South Pole and discovered New Caledonia, South Georgia and many other islands. He also discovered the Hawaiian Islands, which were originally known as the Sandwich Islands.

These achievements made Cook the forerunner of the modern, scientific explorers, and he certainly deserved his fame as one of the greatest British explorers. But unfortunately he was killed in Hawaii in 1779, when his men became involved in fighting with the native Hawaiians.

When it came time for Cook to be reborn a couple of hundred years later, there were actually two or three candidates for his soul. But Soichiro Honda finally won out and received the mandate to carry on Cook's mission of discovery.

As is common knowledge, Honda started out in a small garage in the city of Hamamatsu, but eventually was able to build a world-famous company that sells its products in many nations. His incredible success can be attributed to his rational way of thinking and willingness to always keep challenging the unknown.

And I have come to the conclusion that Captain Cook's exciting life has deeply colored the way Honda has lived his life. His willingness to challenge the unknown is fired by the sub-conscious influence of the soul of the explorer that he was in his previous life. In my mind the images of Captain Cook pouring over his nautical charts and Honda adjusting his blue-prints sometimes overlap.

The sincerity with which Captain Cook undertook his missions is today clearly reflected in the manner with which Honda positively pursues the development of new projects. In other words, because Honda has been able to take advantage of this legacy from the past, he has enjoyed phenomenal luck in his business activities and engineering. Furthermore, if he retains this spirit of exploration and desire to challenge the unknown, there is no reason why Honda's luck should fundamentally change in the days to come. Quite the opposite; his firm should enjoy greater and greater prosperity.

One point of considerable interest in Honda's ties with his previous life is his firm's "English connections." Honda Motor Corp. is today an automobile manufacturer that has carved out its own unique niche in the global automobile market, and its agricultural machinery is also quite well known. But Honda first made its name in motorcycle production and it still is today the world's top two-wheel vehicle manufacturer.

One of the key events that helped it achieve supremacy in the motorcycle field was its victories in the cycle races on the Isle of Man in the Irish Sea. As I am sure you know, the Isle of Man belongs to Great Britain, the motherland of Captain Cook. Only a few years after the company was started Honda managed to win a prestigious motorcycle race there that catapulted into the top ranks of the world's great motorcycle makers. Still today, Honda has many "British connections," including in the fields of joint auto development and local production in the United Kingdom.

In a sense Honda used his victory in the celebrated race on the

Island of Man as a springboard for emulating his illustrious predecessor Captain Cook in conquering the Seven Seas. He has done it in a quite different way, however, shipping his vehicles overseas and actively developing local production activities in foreign countries. I can see the imprint of Captain Cook's temperament active in the subconscious of Soichiro Honda, as it is clearly visible in the way he goes about things.

Well, I have touched on various things concerning Honda's past life as Captain Cook, but I must not forget to point out that the influence of Honda's spiritual protectors cannot be ignored either when discussing his achievements.

The core of Honda's spiritual bodyguard consists of three apparitions of Bishamonten. They are Zuiko Bishamonten, Eiitsu Bishamonten and Sakko Bishamonten. As you will recall, Bishamonten is the god who uses powerful stratagems and clever tactics to vanquish evil and promote good.

Because Honda has been blessed with the backup of these Bishamonten in addition to the explorer's spirit he inherited from his previous existence, he has been a truly lucky individual indeed. On top of that, Honda early on adopted the management philosophy of trying to be helpful to other people. Consequently, the company has grown by leaps and bounds.

CHAPTER 4

Secrets for Acquiring Spiritual Power

Your Star of Good Fortune

Living Money, Dead Money

There are many people in this world who think that good fortune with money simply means the ability to save money. Scrimping and saving, working and slaving, while watching that old bank account balance climb steadily upwards. Those are the preoccupations of a person like that. But then one day just as he is gloating, "Wow! Just look at all the money I've managed to pile up!" without any warning he suddenly drops dead. So all his precious money, which he never even had the opportunity to make use of, becomes the property of the bank. Such laughable scenarios occur all the time.

In such cases, you really have to wonder why these individuals toiled and moiled and saved so assiduously. The point is when a person saves solely for the purpose of saving, his money does neither himself nor anyone else any good. It becomes nothing more than "dead money."

Things might not be so bad if you have your money in a Japanese bank where at least it will earn a little bit of interest. But should it be in a Swiss bank, you will even have to pay a "bank account deposit fee." So if you open up a small account that means that you will either end up making just a little bit of interest or even seeing your principal dwindle down. Such a system is too awful to contemplate!

Money exists to be used. If you ignore this basic principle, then you will never have good luck with money. I explained the correct way to use money in Chapter 1. But I should like to emphasize that "living money" earned in the proper manner should be spent in such a way as to generate happiness for yourself and as many other people as possible. Consider money made in ways that cause other people unhappiness or spent in similar fashion as being taboo.

It is fine to work as hard as you can and save a lot of money. That money should be treated as precious but used as effectively as possible. Like water stored behind a dam, it should be released in liberal quantities as needed. Too much or too little; both methods are wrong. It is important to adjust the release of the water (your use of money) to the needs of any given time. Well, this all seems quite obvious, but...

By the way, do you know what "real money is?" Money can help people or hurt people. "Real money" is the kind that brings joy to people, causes goods to circulate and also serves as a source of happiness for the spiritual world. Every penny is pleasing to the spiritual world if it is put to a constructive use, while billions of dollars that just sit there piled up is of absolutely no use for people, things or the spirits and gods. If you follow my reasoning, it should be obvious to you that even one copper penny has great value if it is earned and spent with true sincerity. If you always treat money that way, then without your even knowing it will become money that is pleasing to the spiritual world and you too will be in its favor. The heart should be the master and money the servant. In other words, if the use of money is under the control of such a pure heart, then it deserves to be called "real money."

You might think that I am belaboring this point, but it is absolutely essential for you to understand this correct way to view money before you ask the stars for good luck with money.

Good Vibrations From the Stars

Those of you who have already read my book *Lucky Fortune* are aware of the "three-tier structure" of the world of the stars. In short, in addition to the material universe in which we exist, there is the *reikai* or spiritual world in which the spirits live, and the divine world, the highest dimension in which the gods reside. As you can see, on some occasions in this book for the sake of simplicity I have been referring to the latter two collectively as the "spiritual world," although in fact they are distinct.

In any event, various kinds of spirits and gods inhabit the bodies in our Solar System, which stretches from the Sun to Pluto. (And of course the other stellar systems are similarly inhabited.) The earth is no exception in that regard. But the inhabitants of our planet are different in that our spirits are clothed in flesh. That is what makes us human.

Now a spirit is capable of sympathetic contact through spiritual vibrations with the flesh, other spirits and even the gods. That is why through study and rigorous spiritual training we can tap into the enormous power of the spirits and gods living on the other bodies in the Solar System.

In fact, even without such special study and training, you can avail yourself of this power to improve your life. You do so through faith. What should you believe in? Nothing other than the "three-tier structure" of the Solar System - the spirits and gods who dwell on its bodies and their inherent power.

Actually, people who have a finely attuned spiritual sense are capable of visualizing the various kinds of good fortune vibrations that emanate from the stars and other celestial bodies. They appear much like the rays of the sun and moon that bathe our earth. If you cannot do so, that simply means that your spiritual mirror is clouded over. But that is no great cause for pessimism.

It is really not necessary for you to see them. All you need to do is believe in them. It is much like the various correct methods for making and spending money that I have described that are guaranteed to bring you good luck with money. You really do not have to know how they work, just that they work! Results are the thing here. And the results you will get will be self-evident.

Now I would like to describe the different good fortune spiritual emanations given off by the Sun and the planets of the Solar System.

The Sun

The Sun is the central source of overall power, which includes good fortune with money. The general pattern here is that it helps you to remain healthy, so that you can work hard and make a lot of money. The Sun of course is the center of the Solar System and the source of energy for all the planets and other satellites. You should tap into the spiritual energy waves of the Sun when you need that extra bit of energy to hang in there on whatever job or task you are engaged in. If you do so, you will find that progress in anything you are doing becomes a lot easier.

Also try using the power call to the Sun Goddess when you are trying to communicate your thoughts. Simply repeat the name "Amaterasu Omikami" eleven times in succession. And even at night when the sun is not out, if you imagine in your mind that it is still shining brightly, have no fear, your prayers will still be heard in the spiritual world of the Sun.

Mercury

This planet emits spiritual vibrations that provide good monetary fortune for those who are engaged in research, doing their utmost on the job and are in search of the truth. You can find the latest Nissan and Toyota models here and many other products of earthly research. Mercury is the planet of engineers, technicians and the most refined artists and craftsmen.

Venus

Venus and money are almost synonymous. In fact, in Chinese characters the name literally means Gold Star. Many people, without even thinking about it, feel an urgent desire to pray fervently to the Morning Star, and that emotion is certainly praiseworthy and natural. That is because Venus is home to both regular gold dragon gods and Yahweh, the protective god of the Jewish people who also happens to be a gigantic gold dragon god. Also there is a special palace here known as the "Money Control Palace," which acts as the nerve center for co-ordinating monetary and corporate policies, national finances and the dissemination of good monetary fortune from Venus. And as its image might well indicate, the type of good fortune delivered by the golden dragon is not the half-way variety of petty piles of cash. It is the kind of good fortune that changes the course of nations, and the world for that matter. This type of good fortune is also attracted to the kinds of power that are wielded by leaders of society like politicians and medical men.

The wondrous powers of Venus are manifested in other ways as well. For example, in an area totally unconnected to monetary fortune, Venus regularly gives rise to revolutionary changes in the sphere of religion. Moses, the Buddha, Jesus Christ and other top religious leaders achieved their successes thanks to the influence of Venus and they reside there now.

Mars

Mars is known as the Fire Star. It is also the celestial body symbolic of war and struggle. It seethes with energy that is constantly flaming up and explosive, furiously attacking power. By tapping into the restless energy of Mars and hooking into its buzzing thought circuits you can win good fortune.

At times when you must attack and vanquish your business rivals, or when you are running low on vitality and enthusiasm, the good fortune vibrations from Mars are just what the doctor ordered. But be forewarned that the type of good fortune delivered by Mars is not the big bucks kind. If you are in need of millions right away, then you better look elsewhere. Here we are talking about the equivalent of what you have earned through your perseverance. I strongly advise professional sportsmen, salesman and others involved in such active, demanding professions to rely on Mars for back up power.

Jupiter

Jupiter is the planet representing prosperity and development, in the form of basic production of goods and the resulting inflow of income. So naturally it is also responsible for corporate prosperity.

Jupiter also helps artists to make money and attract the support of powerful patrons. Make sure you take advantage of the kind of good fortune Jupiter has to offer when you want to motivate people to make money.

I go into this point in greater detail in my book *Lucky Fortune*, but here let me just note that the beautiful "Golden Princess" resides on Jupiter in the "Palace of Gold." If she favors you with her Midas touch, you will be sitting pretty. My firm World Mate organizes Astral Tours that take participants to Jupiter. Of course, we do not go there physically. The *kushimitama* alone is transported to there and other destinations in the spiritual dimension.

Participants on these tours have been able to see conditions on other bodies in our solar system. Actually, the "seeing" too is a bit different from what we are normally used to, since the inhabitants are present in a spiritual dimension invisible to the naked eye. Every time such a tour stops over on Jupiter, the members pray at the a special golden religious center which is actually a shrine, like the Great Shrine at Ise, where worshippers petition for their wishes to come true. Good fortune granted here becomes apparent to the petitioner in anywhere from a day to a few months time when the cash starts pouring in.

Saturn

When Saturn exerts its influence, war is often the result. At least that was what happened in the case of all the major wars Japan has been involved in during modern times – the Sino-Japanese War, the Russo-Japanese War, the First World War and the Second World War.

At heart the denizens of Saturn, including Enma – the King of the Dead, are severe and fond of rigorous training. This is primarily due

to the presence of Enma and the fierce Dosei Konjin of Saturn, which over the ages have spiritually steeled themselves to a fantastic degree. Although in the principles of money making preferred here the emphasis is on economy and the search for efficiency, there is a corresponding lack of warmth and empathy for others. I encourage bankers, stock brokers and other professionals who cannot afford to be too lax in their dealings with the public to tune in to the spiritual power of Saturn. Sampo Kojin, one of the Three Gods of Monetary Fortune whom I described in Chapter II is actually a messenger from Saturn. Of course, Saturn is also home to Sampo Kojin who manifests himself around Mt. Omine and the various peaks, mountains and rivers of our world.

I should not forget to add that good luck for real estate agents and others involved with land also derives primarily from spiritual energy from Saturn, the name for which in Chinese characters means the "Earth Star." In other words, you can develop your fortune and happiness through strenuous activity or dealings concerning land if you pray to the powers of Saturn and act in accordance with the basic tenets of human life.

Uranus

Since I am not authorized to do so by the deities concerned, I will refrain from describing this planet here.

Neptune

Located here is the spiritual world for those who when alive were spiritualists, fortune tellers or had some other kind of special esoteric knowledge. Consequently, the good luck vibrations emanating from here aid those engaged in romantic, imaginative pursuits, such as fiction writers, spiritualists, movie directors, actors and so on. Such people should direct their thoughts and prayers to Neptune. The planet will certainly reward any sincere effort on your part with a swift infusion of spirit power. In other words, this is the most important celestial body for those who would make money from their imagination.

Pluto

The orbit of Pluto usually sets it on the extreme outer limits of the Solar System. Besides being the farthest out of the planets, Pluto also has the role of being the "last" in things. For example, here is located the court that judges the overall worth of a person's life.

The spiritual vibrations from Pluto are especially in tune with the minds of people like examiners, lawyers, police officers and guards, who need to coolly weigh facts, right and wrong, truth and falsehood. That is also true when it comes to good monetary fortune. Those affected by Pluto's vibrations can easily differentiate the good and bad possible effects of their actions and how they are likely to affect others.

Many who have undergone strict spiritual training on Saturn later come to Pluto.

The Moon

The Moon helps bring people happiness. Here dwells the white snake deity who can ensure that you will get the money you need in a true emergency. Salaried company employees, the self-employed and others who pray to the Moon can draw on "white snake power" and thereby stabilize their income and enjoy a happier lifestyle. Finally, let me emphasize that when you are praying to the stars and other celestial bodies, pray to the spiritual world of the Moon last of all. That way you can bring the various prayers into harmony and have the spiritual merit thereby earned converted into real money. By all means, do not forget this point.

The North Star

The world of the North Star is crammed full with spiritual power. Furthermore, since the prayers to the North Star bring enhanced chances that a request will be answered by the spirit world by looking to it for assistance anyone can have his or her talents and capabilities backed up and achieve steadfast good fortune concerning money.

This good monetary fortune provided by the North Star is good in many areas, including academic and cultural pursuits. Moreover, it is extremely stable. So I encourage all my readers to pray for good fortune from this most excellent source.

But let me add one warning. The spiritual powers of the Sun and other celestial bodies are interrelated. But always remember that the Sun is the main actor and the planets and so on supporting actors. Or you might think of the relation in terms of vitamins. The Sun is a multivitamin containing all the important nutrients, while the planets are single vitamins, like Vitamin B12, Vitamin C and so on. They have the original effect of their single ingredient.

Consequently, a proper prayer program should start with prayers to the Sun, followed by prayers to the individual planets, all of which are given greater chance for being answered in a reliable manner by concerted appeal to the North Star. And then this procedure should be wound up by a petition to the Moon, so that the good fortune earned by these prayers may be transformed into real wealth.

Readers who are interested in my spiritual research group World Mate in regards to the Astral Tours or any of our other activities will be sent information free of charge. Kindly write to: World Mate, 3-162 Tachibana Ohitocho, Tagata-gun, Shizuoka, Japan 410-23.

Testimonials to Toshu Fukami

My Relation to Master Fukami

Michihiro Matsumoto
International Communicator

When I am with Master Fukami, I feel a strange sense of tranquillity. If when I am required to go overseas, I first meet with him, I then become enthused about the trip. And I make sure to carry a copy of the Spirit World Logo wherever I go. That alone should be sufficient indication of how his teachings have taken deep root in my soul.

It has already been a decade since I first met Fukami Sensei. He was still quite young then. I was astounded at his spiritual power, as proven by the fact that he got 700 people to show up for one of my speeches in Kyoto. At that time I was not at all acquainted with him, and about all I knew about him was that he was an interesting, indeed awesome leader with a following in Kyoto.

Ten years later when I met Mr. Fukami again he had al- ready become a noted spiritualist. I immediately recognized the enormous spiritual power that he emitted. And I felt that although he was recognized as a foremost medium, he was a person with a sense of humor who could be trusted completely.

After we had known each other for a while, Fukami Sensei was kind enough to appraise my past lives. However, I have to admit I was a bit surprised when he told me that in a past life I had been the famous Zen Buddhist priest Tenkai, who lived in the first part of the Edo Period. Tenkai was the man who as a confidant of Shogun Tokugawa Ieyasu stressed the importance of beliefs like the Seven Divinities of Good Luck.

Oddly enough, even before he spoke to me about my past life, in my writing and public speeches I had repeatedly been saying many of the same things that Tenkai had hundreds of years ago. Even before I made Fukami Sensei's acquaintance, I had been very interested in the spirit world. But he was gracious enough to tell me about my previous life, and explain in detail the interconnection between our material world and the spirit world. As a result I believe my views concerning previous existences and guardian spirits have basically changed.

I like to compare my relationship with Fukami Sensei to a game of *kemari*, the style of football played at the Japanese court in ancient times in which the players skillfully passed the ball with their feet. Likewise, we seem to be able to bounce ideas off each other with the greatest of ease. I can say exactly what I feel with him. And I'm usually in full agreement with his answers. It's great to experience such a perfect meeting of minds.

So ever since I became friends with Fukami Sensei, I have been able to hear all kinds of things about the spirit world from him. Since what he is discussing here is a world in another dimension, and consequently invisible, we cannot actually see any proof about what Fukami Sensei tells us. Perhaps I'm wrong in saying this, but even should everything he says be a big lie, anyone who can tell lies like he does must be a genius. Even if Fukami were a charlatan, you would have to search far and wide to find a person of such intelligence.

Anyhow, the point I am trying to get at is that even if he did not have the special spiritual sensitivity that he does, Fukami would be an extraordinarily charismatic individual.

I Came to Know What I Would Achieve During My Life

Issei Noro
Musician

I first met Fukami Sensei just at a time when I was considering to revamp the way I had thought up till that point and adopt a totally new way of thinking.

My impressions of Fukami the second I first set my eyes on him were: "This is not an ordinary man" and "He has a superhuman quality to him." That is not to say that he looked particularly unusual. As I recall, on that occasion Fukami Sensei was dressed the same as the rest of us present in a tie and business suit. But Fukami Sensei's body seemed to give off some kind of unusual vibes. And we were amazed at the amount of knowledge he had about the gods and Buddha, even though he wasn't the head of any religious organization.

I personally feel that the more I play the guitar, the further I can enter into the world of the gods. I think that's because I am seeking to express the ultimate reality through sounds.

If you asked me whether I believe in any particular religion, I would have to say no. But even at that time I am speaking of, I thought that you have to explain things in such a way that people living in the world today can understand what you are saying. That goes for example for any analysis of the true meaning of the Buddhist sutras, some of which were written down 2,500 years ago.

In that sense I would say that Fukami Sensei is the kind of person who has a special talent for explaining the spirit world in a way that is easy to understand and for conveying the true significance of spiritual matters, including the meaning of the gods and Buddha. I also was convinced by the manner in which Fukami Sensei is able to help us comprehend the essence of human beings, the relationship of the individual to the world, as well as the relationships among various human beings.

I should also mention the time that he explained about my guardian spirit. I remember how he peered straight at my face, but somehow it did not feel like he was really looking at me at all. It was a very strange sensation, I can tell you.

Then he said, "Your guardian spirit is named Dainagon Machioka no Shosho. When he was alive, he was an unsurpassed musician. However, today that guardian spirit will be replaced by Yakuomaru."

That was the very same day that I had firmly decided that even though I wouldn't give up playing the guitar, from that time on I would try to compose the best possible music I was capable of, so that through music I might be able to bring happiness to the people of the world. Then Fukami Sensei added: "Your wonderful sincerity no doubt brought about this change in guardian spirits."

When I heard these words of encouragement, I suddenly felt deep inside that I had been destined to meet Fukami Sensei that day and his words bolstered my confidence in my new way of thinking.

I felt then that Fukami Sensei was teaching me that I had great things to accomplish during my lifetime. And now knowing that I had a strong guardian spirit to watch over me, I became certain that it was up to me to strive my utmost till I had reached this goal.

A Rare Teacher in This World

Satoko Akiyama
Jungian Psychiatrist

Toshu Fukami truly is a most unusual man. The reason I say that is not only is his knowledge of the spirit world very comprehensive, he also never loses sight of this material world. The famous Swiss psychiatrist Carl Jung (1875-1961) once wrote that the healthiest way of living for human beings was to consider the exterior and the interior as being all part of one world at the center of which you stand.

I believe Fukami Sensei does just as Dr. Jung recommended and makes no distinction between the exterior and interior. In other words, he manages to bridge the worlds of reality and vision, and exist very well in a harmonious zone between the two.

A Very Cheerful Psychic

Asami Kobayashi
Media Personality

Fukami Sensei has given to me a dream of another world. I have been very impressed that although he is an extraordinary psychic, he can be startlingly cheerful.

Toshu and I Are "Childhood Friends"

Robert Shields
Pantomimist

(Robert Shields has appeared on Japanese TV commercials and has been named by Michael Jackson as America's number one pantomimist.)

Fukami Sensei's boundless love makes it possible for him to draw out the *child* that is inside each of us. I consider myself very lucky for having met him.

We get along like childhood buddies. Our personalities complement each other perfectly. Yeah, the trustful vibes are just like those you get with childhood playmates. What do I think about Fukami? – He's a gift from God – He's a beacon of light – His vision transcends this world.

For myself, and indeed everyone, he is the *Master Light Maker* – that is the "supreme commander" who directs the light of hope in our direction. Just to be together with him is an overwhelming joy. Even though he is naturally an amateur when it comes to pantomime, if I jump into an improvisational pantomime routine, Fukami Sensei will respond immediately with one of his own. You see, he's able to communicate effectively via the supra-verbal form of mime. I don't know anyone besides Fukami Sensei with whom I can carry on and have fun like this for hours.

In other words, Fukami Sensei is a natural. He can freely control his body and mind. He's really amazing. On top of that, he's got the ability to understand the inner world.

Japan is too materialistic these days. I think it is very significant that Fukami Sensei should be instructing us about the world of the spirit at a time like this.

The world we live in is really nothing but an illusion. I think that Fukami Sensei is trying to tell us that it is nothing but a school, or training ground if you like, to prepare us for the spirit world and our future lives. I think there are only two things that we will be able to take with us when we go: love and the wisdom we have acquired while on earth.

Fukami Sensei, thanks so much for feasting me. If you can make it to Arizona, I'll be more than happy to return the favor. But with my "cuisine" no matter how much you eat you'll never get fat. Why? That's because I serve up pantomime.

Selected Prayers

The Three Gods of Good Fortune
Ritual for Worshipping Sampo Kojin

Place pine sprigs on both sides of the house shrine.

If you do not have pine, *sakaki* is fine too. It is best to change these offerings on the first and the fifteenth of each month. Change the water every morning.

Place three long sticks of incense to the left of the shrine as you face it. Place cleaned rice in the dish to the right and salt in the one on the left. Open the lid of the receptacle, as shown in the illustration.

After reciting the Amatsu ritual prayer that follows this explanation, offer a prayer in your own words.

If you follow these procedures every single morning, the effectiveness of the prayers will be greatly enhanced.

The accompanying illustration shows the shrine or residence of the divinity Sampo Kojin.

When also worshipping Sanmen Daikokuten and Zao Gongen, it is appropriate to worship all three deities together, since they all are manifestations of gods or Buddhas from Japan's divine world.

The power call for Zao Gongen is:

Onsa bendara yaasowaka

The one for Daikokuten is:

Onmaka gyaaraa yaasowaka

Of course, it is perfectly all right to use the Amatsu Norito, normal prayers and the power calls together at one time. Just make sure your soul is serene and your hands are joined solemnly.

It is possible to simply imagine in your heart the accompanying illustration, and consider the shrine as jointly dedicated to Sampo Kojin, Sanmen Daimokuten and Zao Gongen, when repeating the power calls. Such a procedure will bring you a certain amount of spiritual power. However, when you must call forth as much spiritual power as you possibly can, it is best to worship in front of a proper shrine where the gods are embodied.

If there is no shrine that inspires your confidence near you or you do not have your own home shrine, please contact World Mate, Tel: 0558-76-1060, Fax: 0558-76-1158. Proper shrines containing the spirits of the gods can be provided to the faithful at a moderate charge.

Amatsu Norito

Oh ye God and Goddesses who dwell in the High Heavenly Plain of Takaamahara,

To you I humbly address these auspicious words in accordance with your dictates.

Izanagi no Okami, ancestor of the Imperial Line was the first deity to appear in this world.

When after emerging from the polluted land of Yomi (Hades), he bathed and purified himself at the river mouth on the Plain of Awagi near Tachibana-no-Odo in Hyuga on the island of Tsukushi, the gods who control purification were born.

We address ye the Gods of Heaven and the Gods of Earth and ask you to purify and rectify the myriad mistakes, errors, sins and impurities of this world.

Thus we address all the gods and goddesses with the profoundest respect and awe, asking that our humble request be heeded.

Tokoto no Kajiri

Ama-terasu-o-mi-kami (Say eleven times)

Sampo Kojin

O, Sampo Kojin protect us against the devils to the fore and the devils to the rear, and grant us your blessings.

(Say twice)

We humbly thank you for protecting the kitchen accounts.

(A continuation after the first part is said twice)

Zao Gongen

O, Zao Gongen protect us and grant us your blessings. (Say twice)

Thank you for furnishing us with various forms of worldly wisdom and for helping our sales grow briskly.

(A continuation after the first part is said twice)

Sanmen Daikokuten

O, Sanmen Daikokuten, protect us and grant us your blessings.
(Say twice)
Thank you for circulating good fortune from person to person.
(A continuation after the first part is said twice)

Hints on How to Enjoy Good Luck With Money and Make It in the World

1. The Tamafuri Method

It is not good to use techniques like ESP simply out of curiosity, but if the purpose is to become closer to the gods, bring happiness to other people or raise the spiritual level of your soul, then their use is certainly justified. That is because if you do something to improve yourself or others, it is in accordance with the way of the gods. I would first like to make this point very clearly. However, should you use ESP in a half-joking manner, it is possible that devils will respond and without your even being aware of it cause disasters for you. I implore you to be very careful in this regard, since otherwise you could find yourself unable to lead a normal life or even going mad.

You can use the *Tamafuri* or soul-dissimulation Method to increase your psychic powers. The first step is to concentrate and seek to create a wealth of clear images in your mind. That is because the power of these images can be converted into spiritual

power. *Tamafuri* actually amounts to image-dissimulation or flinging away of the *Kushimitama*.

But mere training through image power is also a yoga technique. So there is nothing special to be found here. That is insufficient to draw forth a correct response from the divine world. Your images must incorporate feelings of true love and sincere, totally honest

prayers. If they do not, then they will amount to nothing more than the black magic technique of "power up training" centered on the ego, and this will earn you punishment in the afterworld.

For a detailed discussion of this problem, kindly consult my book *Divine Powers*.

Incidentally, when you create images you should strive for them to be as *life-like* as possible. For example, if you are conjuring up an "ocean" try to make it so realistic that the briny smells of the open sea will tickle your nostrils. It might help in this regard to draw pictures of the image you have in mind or study a bit about art.

I got this bit of information directly from Kukai (Kobo Daishi) when I established spiritual contact with him. He told me that the real reason he painted and sculpted when he was alive was that he

wanted to increase his level of spiritual power and strengthen his powers of image realization. These activities also apparently helped to increase and prolong his powers of concentration in general. His explanation seemed perfectly appropriate to me when I heard it.

Apparently Kukai was thinking that by painting and sculpting he would not only be able to raise his own level of aesthetic appreciation, he would also become capable of creating mandalas, which really are one form of representation of the divine world, that would be of use in the spiritual training of his disciples in the generations to come. Likewise, the statues he sculpted also provided images of the deities for worship. So his artistic activities really amounted to a case of killing three birds with one stone in regards to ascetic training of the spirit.

In this regard I might note that I myself draw pictures of Mt. Fuji on *shikishi*, a special kind of paper used for writing poems on. This is a mystical method for transferring some of the spiritual energy from the divine world on Japan's most sacred mountain. Such pictures are referred to as "Wind-Generating Pictures."

You probably will not believe me when I tell you this, but these pictures are really a form of super-advanced talismatic art and the *shikishi* on which the representations of Mt. Fuji have been drawn actually does give off a gentle breeze. And of course these pictures bring a lot of luck to the owner. I know several artists, models and actresses who are big fans of this kind of art.

The kind of superhuman powers involved in art and bringing good fortune are more advanced than those used for things like setting kindlewood on fire with the mind. And they are also quite modern, since you can hang these pictures up in your own home. They are also conducive to dreaming.

Well, let us return from this tangent to the question of the methods for releasing the soul through the use of imagination. What happens if they do indeed allow you to perceive a large number of images. For one thing you will start getting clear images of Shinto shrines. But the first thing you need to do is visit a shrine in whatever area you happen to be in, and if at all possible the first shrine to have been established in that locale, so that you can get the image firmly fixed in your mind.

Why should you be visiting Shinto shrines? That is because these are the homes of the tutelary or guardian gods of a particular area. These gods play all kinds of roles, including having the responsibility to guide us in all kinds of things from good fortune in work, to marriage and luck with money. They also serve as our guides to the spirit world. So as you can see. As a matter of fact, these tutelary gods are supremely important in matters affecting our daily lives.

Ideally, you should visit their shrines every single day. But of course that is impossible for many people, what with the hectic pace of their daily lives, the lack of one of these shrines in their neighborhood and other factors. In such a case what you need to do is imagine such a shrine in your head, indicate your desire to pay an actual visit to it and then offer to the resident deities the sincerest prayer you are capable of.

The life-like image and your sincere faith will thus be able to overcome problems of space and distance and you will draw a response from the divine dimension. When you are imagining such a shrine try to conjure up as many of the details of an actual shrine as possible: the *torii* gate and gravel path leading to the sacred precincts, the sacred trees on both sides of the path, the style of the main shrine building and so on.

Also, to reaffirm your belief in the resident gods repeat the *norito* prayer given earlier three to five times, the *tokoto no kajiri* eleven times and also repeat the following phrase several times, "Oh, you, the tutelary deity of this shrine, grant me your blessings." Then you

can add your own personal prayer for whatever you are asking for. If you repeat this procedure every single day, I will guarantee that you become quite sensitive spiritually.

Well, it really goes without saying that it is strictly taboo to use your ESP skills for evil or selfish purposes that totally center on your own happiness. At all times, you should maintain a manner of thinking rigorously attuned to the way of the gods. In other words, it is important for your innermost being to be thinking constantly: "I desire that which is best for myself and others. May all be made proper. I leave the results up to the gods."

If you act in this fashion, then you will steadily develop correct ESP powers.

Finally, I would like to provide a word of warning concerning shrines or temples where no god resides, but which instead have been invaded by evil spirits. I explain how to spot such places in *Lucky Fortune.*

2. Get the Spirits to Help You When Dealing With Tough Bosses and Clients

If you want to get ahead in the world, it is essential that you learn the trick of learning how to handle bosses or clients whom you cannot stand without ruffling their feathers. Catering to the wishes of such people can be humiliating and disagreeable at times, but if you utilize the secret methods for gaining the understanding of the spirit world that I will outline below, you will find that you can get along just fine with anyone.

The key rationale when using these methods is that before you actually meet the individual in question, you must explain the circumstances to his guardian deity, protective spirits and the *mitama* (soul). If you follow this procedure, then when you meet him you might be surprised to discover you do not feel a bit agitated or exasperated and that everything seems to go very smoothly.

"Is what you're saying for real?" many dubious people are certain to counter. But all I ask is that such people give it a try just one time. For example, say you are in a situation where it is clear that you are in the right and the other fellow is completely wrong, but you still have to bow and scrape to him.

Just try remembering that just like you this other guy has a reason to be on earth – a mission of his own from the gods. Also recall that he has his own guardian spirits. So even if you cannot respect him as a human being, respect these guardian spirits. Imagine that you are really bowing your head to these guardian spirits not him. If you do, then showing signs of respect to the detested individual will no longer gall you. And in turn, the other fellow's guardian spirits will be receptive to you. And when you actually get together with this guy, everything will go smoothly. Furthermore, the other person will thereby naturally recognize that he was wrong. It will be a case of his soul responding to the sense of decorum that you have displayed.

Well then, let me introduce this secret method. Start by repeating the following formula more than ten times with all of the sincerity at your command: "O, guardian deities, protective spirits and the *mitama* (soul) of Mr. (use the name of the individual.)"

While doing so, have faith that these three kinds of spirits are indeed present where you are at. Faith increases the level of response from the spirit world several times over.

Next, while keeping the lessons of the mandala in mind, conjure up in your mind the images of the individual's guardian spirits and the guardian deities behind them, as well as the *mitama* provided with the face of the individual (it is also all right to substitute the image of a shining jewel) and address them in as much detail as possible. By all means, do not forget to pray with great sincerity, finishing off with the request that "Mr. X and myself as well be led to the good." Also add: "Should I be in the wrong, let me know through the words of Mr. X. I humbly beg your help in this matter."

The guardian spirits operate the same for others as they do for you. And you do not have to limit your prayers to your own guardian spirits. If you can adopt the broad perspective, then there is no reason why the guardian spirits of others will be reluctant to lend you assistance as well. So you can end up having your own guardian spirits and the guardian spirits of others combining as your allies. This is an excellent, secret method for increasing the guardian spirit power backing you up.

Naturally, before you pray to another's guardian spirits, you need to explain the situation fully to your own guardian spirit. This in effects helps you to build bridges to the spirit world. It is the "secret method for obtaining the understanding of the spirit world."

It goes without saying that your guardian spirits are not evil gods or evil spirits, nor can they be deceived. So they will refuse to work on your behalf unless you call upon them with real sincerity and wish the best for both yourself and others. Furthermore, if things

work out as you want them to, you must be sure to thank these spirits from the bottom of your heart. This is absolutely vital if you want them to respond positively the next time you come around seeking help.

Lest I forget, there is another caveat in regards to the use of this secret method. That is never, never pray only for the concrete results of your desires. The guardian spirits are of such a nature that

they are capable of seeing the past, present and future as one seamless fabric. Also, from their vantage point in the spirit world, they are well aware of the correct standards of good and evil.

By asking for specific results, you are in effect setting yourself up as the judge and jury about what is right for you. In other words, you end up running around like a riderless horse, confirmed in your own perversity and egotistical thoughts and opinions. You inevitably end up running off in a different direction from the true results that the spiritual world intends for you.

So what you need to do, even if you can more or less foresee the results, is to pray in the following manner: "I have faith that in the end the best possible results will come my way. But if possible dear gods and spirits, could you arrange things in such a way that I myself and the others concerned will all benefit spiritually. I promise to do my very best, and I leave the rest up to your will."

This is the kind of prayer you need to offer – one that promises the best effort on your part and at the same time leaves the final outcome up to the spirit world. If you conduct yourself in this manner, the spirit world will put out that much more in your behalf and you are likely to enjoy results better than you had hoped for. The reason for that is that because the spiritual clouds created by your own overweening ego have dissipated and you have managed to gain some control of your own mitama, your band of guardian deities is ready and willing to give their all for your cause.

Lastly, I would like to introduce some techniques that should help you in the workplace.

1. Pray in the hallways when no one is around.

2. When too many people are around the workplace to make prayer possible, retire to the restroom and lock yourself in a stall for your own private prayer session. If somebody is in the stall next to you, then flush the toilet to drown out the sound of your praying.

3. When you knock on the door of a superior or at the office of a client, think of it as a signal to convey greetings to the guardian spirit of the person inside. When you bow to another, consider it as a greeting to that person's guardian spirits, protective deities and *mitama*. If you act in this way, in an amazing number of cases your superior or the other person involved will respond very favorably to you.

4. Employ the power call for improving human relations, *Senten namu furuhobiru* just before you begin an appointment, repeating it over and over softly to yourself. If possible, say it thirty-six times.

224

5. When another person is bawling you out, do not display any strong emotion, but in your heart say the same power call. This will cut off the other person's anger as soon as possible.

I trust that you will carefully study the above suggestions, take them to heart and by all means use them. You will see for yourself just how effective they can be. If you understand the basic principles involved, then these secret techniques can be applied in any number of situations. For example in quarrels with spouses or siblings, in times of discord with friends or lovers, when there are complaints or claims from clients, and so on. In all these circumstances, these techniques will prove very powerful.

These secret techniques will not cause unhappiness for anyone and will instead steadily extend the ring of happiness. So I hope that all of my readers will acquire the knack for using them in their daily lives.

Swiss Thinking About Money

Switzerland is of course a mountain-locked nation. Its residents are known for their very logical sense of thrift. The Swiss have not taken very much to the philosophy of selling a great deal with a small profit margin. Instead local industries uniformly try to sell their products for ten times the unit production costs, while not polluting the beautiful countryside. Furthermore, the Swiss treat their consumer goods carefully, so that they can continue to be used for a long period of time. Consequently, all the autos you see on the roads are sparkling clean. The Swiss like things even cleaner than the Japanese, who are well known for their fastidiousness. That national characteristic is behind the success of the famous Swiss watch.

Why should this be so? The reason was quite clear to me when I visited Switzerland. The country is covered with deep mountain folds and dramatic differences in elevation of a national topography seem to be duplicated in miniature in the brains of the highly intelligent Swiss people which are deeply creased from much thought.

Normally people who grow up in rural areas where fruits and vegetables are plentiful tend to be gentle and genial. But a look at Japanese history shows that such areas also tend to produce very intelligent and logical sons. For example the famous warlord Takeda Shingen hailed from the mountainous province of Kai or what is now Yamanashi Prefecture to the southwest of Tokyo. The famous Iga and Koga *ninja* and Omi merchants also came from such areas in what are now Mie and Shiga prefectures.

All these people shared certain personality traits, including perseverance and very logical thinking. It is frequently said that a severe natural environment makes the people who have to survive amidst it brighter. There are exceptions, however. The deep wisdom of the Russian people is no doubt at least partly explained by this factor. Also, Nagano Prefecture, which is roughly synonymous with the Japan Alps region, is known for the high standards of education it has long maintained. Many people here are good with figures. So in many ways the residents of Nagano are similar to the Swiss who of course live in the real Alps. There are also common points between the types of industrial goods produced and patterns of development in the two areas.

The typography of a region also has a great effect on the local spiritual world. For better or worse, the souls of the individuals are shaped by the place where they were born. And conversely, in many cases a person is born into an area that ,matches the personal idiosyncrasies of his or her soul.

Anyhow, in discussing Switzerland and the relation to good material fortune, I think we should point out that there are many things we could learn from the Swiss. Probably the most important is the virtue of thriftiness.

It should be pointed out in the first place that there are basically two methods of saving money. One is to get money to come in. The other is to make sure that it does not go out. In the latter case, the motive should not be greed but rather an endeavor of logic. That is when thrift becomes a true virtue. In that sense Switzerland is certainly worthy of the title of the thriftiness nation in the world.

The psychologist Satoko Akiyama told me this story about a Swiss professor who once visited Japan. In order to save money on lodging, the professor remodeled a storeroom at Dr. Akiyama's home. Not only that. He also was extremely careful about his expenditures on food. He diligently checked out all the cheap Chinese restaurants in the neighborhood that catered to penny-pinching students, comparing the prices and volume of *gyoza* fried dumplings as well as *ramen* noodles, and their price and ingredients. He meticulously jotted down all this assiduously acquired data into a notebook and then compared volume, prices and taste before making up a list of his top picks. It was amazing. Dr. Akiyama recalls how one time when she wanted to have a cup of tea and put the kettle on the fire, the professor came running and said, "Don't act so wastefully. You're wasting a lot of water if you only want to have one cup." He then carefully measured out the amount of water and carefully watched the flame till the water had just started boiling. Then he killed the flame, filled exactly one teacup full with the liquid and handed it to Dr. Akiyama.

We Japanese consider the waste of time or labor to be awful, but the Swiss seem to be even more advanced when it comes to treating things as being precious. Even the most fanatically thrifty Japanese could learn something from this Swiss professor. And just think, at

one point the good professor even told Dr. Akiyama, "I would be considered rather profligate in my habits compared to most Swiss." Have mercy!

Actually, the penchant of the Swiss for being so "cheap" and their frugal ways are the direct result of the influence of Jurojin, who you will remember is one of the Seven Divinities of Good Luck. As I explained earlier, Jurojin embodies the virtue of thrift and his long, long head symbolizes the vast wisdom acquired from his continuing efforts towards logical thinking. That is one of the reasons why Switzerland could be called the greatest nation when it comes to respect for the ideals of Jurojin. Prices are also stable there with little inflation, and it has many very wealthy citizens.

Switzerland might be considered a model case at the national level of how thoroughgoing frugality is an open invitation for good fortune to come knocking. Unfortunately, the Japanese people these days seem ready to throw away still usable televisions and refrigerators at the drop of a hat. I think we should take the example of the "Jurojin Swiss" to heart and become a little more reluctant to waste things. That holds especially true for those people who are always making complaints like, "Yeah, we make enough, but we never seem to be able to save anything."

Good Fortune Through the Horoscope

All natural phenomenon can be attributed to the interaction of the five elements of fire, wood, earth, metal and water. And the nine tendencies that are observable in their interaction form the basis of the horoscope system known in Japan as kyuseigaku. It was developed by a man named Shinjiro Sonoda, who based it on traditional Chinese techniques of divination that date back thousands of years. The resulting Japanese-style horoscope system has gained popularity since the Taisho Period in the 1920s. Although superficially the system might seem easy for anyone to understand and use, actually I cannot think of anything else on earth that is as difficult to grasp in depth.

Be that as it may, I would like to give a very simple introduction to the different influences that the nine horoscope signs have on good luck with money. But let me make it clear once again I am a spiritualist; I am not a practitioner of aspect divination. Of course, it would be a pleasure for me to explain all of this in terms of the spirit powers, but if I did so I would end up writing another entire book here. So I will merely touch on the bare rudiments of the question. In fact, I have already ended up writing a rather long introduction to what I want to say on this point. Let us get into the heart of the matter, shall we?

What this horoscope system basically does is judge a person to be under the influence of one of nine stars depending on the year in which he was born. By knowing that we can decide what general personality categories he should be fitted into. Take a look at the positive aspects given for your own star below. By carefully considering the positive aspects indicated by your controlling star you should be able to get some idea about what good effects in the area of good monetary fortune you can look forward to.

One White Water Star – This star in the west promises subsidiary income and gold. The emphasis here is on money made in the shadows rather than on center stage. The *one white* in the star's name actually means water. In Japan the term *mizu shobai* refers to night life service businesses like bars, cabarets and so on, most of which make their money through the sale of alcoholic beverages. This is the star that governs the good luck of people in that sort of business.

Two Black Earth Star – This star promises stable income. Operating income will grow steadily. Jobs should be selected that call for regular dealings with the general public.

Three Green Wood Star – This star is connected with showy promotion and publicity. The "green wood" refers to spring. This is the star of discovery and development, creativity and growth. So if this is your lucky star, get involved in showy work that involves the use of the voice and sounds.

Four Green Wood Star – With this star the emphasis is on trust. If you can work as a go-between for people then the money will come pouring in. Develop honor and trustworthiness; avoid recklessness.

Five Yellow Earth Star – With this star the emphasis is on perseverance. If you just hang in there, without a shadow of a doubt eventually the day you receive your reward will arrive. The type of person who is governed by this star is basically the "commander type," who almost maternally will nurture the growth of people and things and thereby achieve success. However, be advised that these tendencies can in extremes become the "five yellows killing tendency." Also this is not a lucky orientation for everyone.

Six White Metal Star – People who are governed by this star have a good chance of getting rich. Monetary luck is good for those in professions where they manage others or where they are looked up to by others. You may get assistance from your father or another source, or you may be in charge of public funds. If you handle money entrusted to you carefully, you should enjoy potent monetary luck.

Seven Red Metal Star – An alternative name might be the Monetary Fortune Star. The orientation is westward. If you can learn to laugh and control your tendency to feel mistreated then wealth should pour in.

Eight White Earth Star – This star controls good fortune in regards to businesses dealing with real estate or other real property and things. Also, if you pay due attention to your family and other human relationships, then without even thinking about it good luck with money should be yours.

Nine Violet Fire Star – This star governs good fortune for aesthetic things. The "nine violet" signifies "the highest" and "god." Therefore it is concerned with religious affairs. It also affects good luck regarding written documents, education, the arts and similar things.

Well, in very, very general terms I have explained above the general tendencies of the nine stars in the *kyusei* system as they affect good luck with money. But as I mentioned earlier, this form of astrology is actually quite deep and complicated. Furthermore, the better versed you become in it, the more frightening things become – which is to say that the disasters and bad luck you run into far outweighs the auspicious side of things.

Consequently, in order to become skillful in manipulating "aspect divination" you have to believe actively in the positive aspects of things and make practical use of them, while at the same time refusing to believe in bad things. If you accept the evil aspects, your thoughts and conduct will as a matter of course tend in the negative direction. So your chances for good luck will necessarily diminish.

Palmistry That Ensures Good Fortune

"**I** work and slave, but still cannot lead a decent life. I just sit and stare at my hands." All the time you hear lots of people complaining like this.

Well, what exactly do you get if you look at a person's hands? A lesson in palmistry, that is what. Maybe in such a case you will see that this person in question really does not have a decent good fortune line so that it seems no matter whatever they might do they

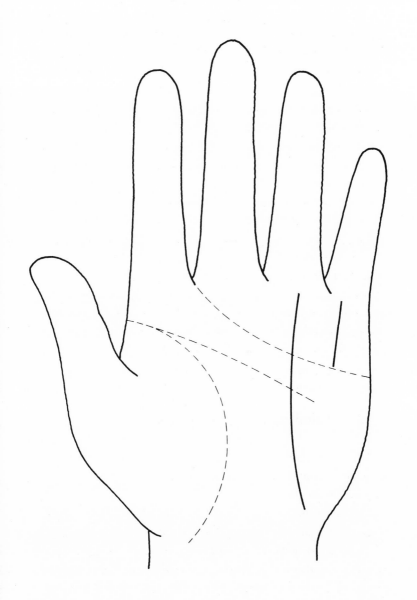

are not destined to become wealthy. But in other instances, there will be a very healthy good fortune line. Then you can encourage the person to hang in there by telling him that if he does, he has good future hopes. Well, in any event I encourage you to try your own good fortune palmistry based on the power of positive thinking.

The principles involved are really quite simple. All you really need to do it is a ball pen or magic marker to trace out the fortune lines on your hand.

But this is not just a case of your tracing what you see. While doing so, you have to say to yourself quite emphatically: "I am going to have good monetary fortune for sure. No, I already have it. I have been blessed with good monetary fortune; I am a lucky, happy individual."

But make sure that you do not have any negative thoughts at all, like, "Is this guy for real?" "I'll get my hand dirty" or "What if somebody sees me?" Perish such thoughts from your mind.

The science of palmistry is designed to help you understand the deepest levels of your subconscious. Like the ancient oracle methods of reading the cracks in heated tortoise shells and deer bones for portents, the lines and crevices of the hand are normally read for signs about the future.

The secret method I am teaching here works in the opposite fashion, however. In other words, you add new lines to the natural patterns on your palm that reflect the current state of your subconscious, so as to reflect the way that you would like to see your future develop. Then you will these changes with all your might. The goal is to influence favorably the arayashiki, the deepest level of the subconscious and the part of the spiritual world that handles concepts.

Any number of people have successfully employed this strategy in the past, so that is why I am recommending this technique here. The funny thing is that the places that you first outlined with the ball pen or marker come to resemble real lines and wrinkles. You cannot help but feel that the mysterious workings of the lowest levels of the human subconscious are at work here. This technique should of course always be used to increase your personal happiness, but never at the cost of unhappiness for others. Use it while trusting in goodness, having firm faith that your luck will change for the better and with complete confidence.

A fundamental law of the spirit world is that if the power for improving the deepest levels of the subconscious is boosted, then the fortune of the individual concerned will also take a turn for the better.

Lack of confidence and lack of action go hand in hand and in tandem they guarantee that you will never enjoy good luck with money. So when you trace your palm, do it with conviction and unswerving confidence!! This is very important. It should be pointed out that in palmistry there are several different schools. In my explanation I am relying on the *Ryunen* Method developed by Yasuto Nishitani.

I do not wish to keep repeating the same point, but since this is probably the first time that you have traced your palm, I would reiterate that if you have the necessary confidence and undertake this experiment with willingness and the intention to do it right, the result will be an accurate reading of your own palm will take on the desired fortune lines.

Basically a palm analysis is intended to tell about the prospects for good fortune and the overall fate of the owner, as well as his past, present and future and his spiritual background. But strangely enough when done properly, that is with the person undergoing the analysis exerting the full force of his will and cooperating completely, the future direction of the palms lines can also be modified.

In other words, it is blatantly wrong to say that the condition of everyone's palm is fixed and immutable. New lines can be incised and old lines miraculously disappear.

You can see the lines promising good fortune steadily in- crease in number and those that indicate the seeds of ill fortune gradually disappear. Here I am offering you a method for making your palm luckier and it is a tried and proven method too. It is something that can actually improve your lot. Human beings should not just leave their destinies up to the whims of Fate. The laws of the spiritual world dictate that if a person tries as hard as he can every single second, he can improve his fated lot in life. I have explained the rationale behind this in *Lucky Fortune* and other books of mine. The important point here is that the secret palmistry method represents one valid way in which this principle can be applied.

But you might ask, "Should I trace on my right hand or my left hand?" The answer is the right one. The reason why is that the right hand represents the present Will of Heaven. The left hand represents the Will of Heaven at the time of your birth. In other words, the right hand reflects specific and concrete changes. The changes that are shown on the left hand are primarily psychological in nature.

If you can understand these basic principles, you can vigorously trace the monetary good luck and wealth lines with full confidence and faith. Those who are interested in a full exposition of this method of palmistry should consult Mr. Nishitani's book *Palmistry Revolution* or *An Introduction to Palmistry* (published by Nihon Bungeisha).

Good Fortune Logos

Divine Logos. The logos of the divine world are special marks capable of making the power of the spiritual world available to you. You might view them as one mechanism for receiving and focusing the divine power at the spot on earth where you are. The divine logos that I have made public up till this point were all learned directly from the gods, when my soul was on astral voyages through the Andromeda Galaxy and to other planets. I received the special permission of the divine world to teach others about logos that have actually been used to make effective use of divine power. So you can use them with complete confidence and peace of mind.

Faith is Vital. As I explained in detail in *Lucky Fortune,* the logos of the divine world will call forth divine power that can vary greatly in intensity depending upon the faith and strength of thinking of the person who is repeating them. I urge you to have the greatest faith when looking at the logo. Tell yourself: *Power from the divine world has already come to me* or *I truly possess good monetary fortune*. In this frame of mind stare at a given logo steadily for at least one full minute so that the impression will be burned into the back of your brain.

Keep Near You. Besides firmly fixing the impression of the logo in your mind, you should place copies of the divine logo in all necessary places. For example, place copies of divine logos to promote business, to keep your mind from thinking in scatterbrain fashion, to stimulate the wisdom needed to discover the truth and to create new ideas and products in prominent places in your office like the conference room and the president's office. You should also place them on your desk. Or you might make small copies to

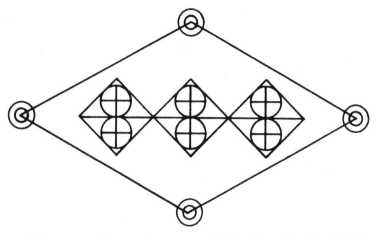

stick in your wallet or other personal belongings. My firm World Mate has available silver and gold plates with these divine logo on them, as well as badges and pendants you can wear on your person at all times, and other items with the logos on them. (For further information call 0558-76-1060)

Incidentally, gold items greatly encourage the manifestation of spiritual power in the material dimension, while silver ones do likewise for the psychological dimension. The reason why most of the logo items offered by World Mate are made with either gold or silver is that we want to ensure happiness for people in both these important dimensions of human life. All of these designs and trademarks for World Mate's logos have been registered, so that although individuals are free to use them as they desire any commercial resale is forbidden by law.

The income that World Mate earns from the sale of these logo items goes to a fund that supports welfare projects for the elderly, aid for refugees and youth education activities.

Be Serious. Be well aware that these divine logos possess a great deal of power. They are not to be trifled with. But if you employ them in the correct frame of mind – wishing good for yourself, your neighbors and the divine world - then they can bring you explosively good luck. On the other hand, if you are obsessed with good fortune only for yourself and completely disregard any ill fortune you might cause to others during the process when you make use of these logos, then you will be courting the wrath of Heaven. And when you die and go to the spiritual world, punishment and suffering will be waiting for you. Naturally, it is also taboo to use these logos in a jesting, irreverent manner.

Combine With Power Calls. The power calls are special incantations capable of bringing forth powerful spiritual emanations from the divine world. If you use the divine logos in conjunction with these power calls, the resulting good luck and good fortune with money will be doubled in effect. Thinking of this double-barrel approach as something to be used when the circumstances call for it – as in an emergency or when time needs to be saved.

Wealth Logo. The illustration above shows the special logo designed to attract material wealth to you. It is referred to as the Monetary Fortune Invitation Logo. To use it, cross your hands together and place the little finger of each hand on the double circles on each side of the diagram.

Do so. Then think to yourself with full faith, "Good fortune with money is on the way." I guarantee that if you do so, good fortune will indeed come to you.

The Divine Logo to Drive Out Evil and Welcome Good and the Diagram for Calling Good Monetary Fortune should be used in the same pure frame of mind.

WORLD MATE

World Mate is a unique organization with members of all ages, which strives to perfect an ever expanding circle of happiness with the ultimate goal of realizing the paradise on earth that the divine world desires for humanity. This is accomplished by enhancing communication among people and between them and the divine world.

As a reflection of its fresh, dynamic approach to the quest for fulfillment in life, World Mate engages in a wide range of activities in the fields of education, social welfare, art, cultural interchange and sports in Japan and overseas. These are very much in line with the group's basic philosophy that an individual can only achieve real happiness and self-realization if he expresses gratitude to his guardian spirits and divine benefactors and helps make others happy.

In addition to seminars and diverse spiritual activities, some of which are directly participated in by senior advisor Toshu Fukami, World Mate issues a newsletter and other publications for its members, and offers for sale books and tapes by Fukami and sacred items used in ritual observances, such as Divine Good Fortune Logos.

World Mate currently has over 80 branches located in every part of Japan. One of the greatest joys of membership in World Mate is the opportunity to interact with other members, who tend to be young, well-educated, highly attractive people.

It should also be noted that in its stress on the expression of free will, World Mate fundamentally differs from coercive "new religions" or dark occult groups.

Profile

Haruhisa Handa—Toshu Fukami

Mr. Handa was born in 1951 and graduated from Doshisha University with a degree in Economics in 1976. In 1977 he founded Misuzu Corporation which has several different operating divisions. One division has been running a small-class prep school for 15 years. At present it has more than 4,000 students and employs 450 qualified teachers. The school has been recognized in Japan as number one in its category.

The trading division is well-known as a manufacturer and wholesaler of watches, producing its own brand of watches. It has a range of about 3,000 items, imports goods to Japan from Europe, the U.S. and Hong Kong, and will soon be importing goods from Australia. Misuzu has retail shops in all the major department stores in Japan including Seibu, Takashimaya, Mitsukoshi, Daimaru and others. The company has been recognized as number one in its field.

Mr. Handa also established Tachibana Shuppan Co. Ltd. This is a publishing house which has published many books on varied topics including sports, religion, philosophy and language. Measured by profit growth, Tachibana was the number three publishing house in Japan in 1991.

Mr. Handa is an author, artist, musician, composer and poet. His pen name is Toshu Fukami. He has written 15 books which have sold a total of around 2,000,000 copies. The theme of his books is to fuse spiritualism with practical business. He is a poet of Japanese *Waka* and writes popular songs. He loves music and enjoys playing the piano and violin and also singing opera. He aims to revive classical art and is a composer of piano music, symphonies, opera and ballet music.

In Japan he is well known as a motivational speaker and holds at least three seminars a month, which are attended by between 2,500 and 3,000 people each. In keeping with his aim to support art, he recently engaged the Australian pianist, David Helfgott to perform in Japan at one of his seminars, and will continue to invite artists whose work may not be widely known in Japan.

In 1990, his personal qualities, abilities and important contributions in so many fields were recognized by Honolulu University, which awarded him with an Honorary Degree of Doctor of Divinity. Their accompanying comment was, "We need him and his talent in the next century."

Mr. Handa is one of the world's major sponsors of blind golf. Some of the golf tournaments for which he has been the main sponsor or has committed himself to be so are: Australian Open Golf Championship for the Blind and Visually Impaired (1989-1998 inclusive), British Open Blind Golf Championship (1991, 1992), World Blind Golf Championship (1990, 1992, 1994, 1996), Nedlands Masters Professional Golf Tournament (1989, 1990, 1991). In addition, Mr. Handa recently formed the first Japanese Blind Golf Association which was built on the foundation of the World Mate Blind Golf Club which began four years earlier. Mr. Handa is a forerunner promoting the blind golf movement in Japan, and is sponsoring many events in that country.

Mr. Handa also endows the Toshu Fukami Scholarship at Curtin University to promote cultural exchanges between Australia and Japan. The endowment for this scholarship is $1,000,000 for a period of ten years. He has also given significant support to various Western Australian charity organizations.

Major Toshu (Seizan) Fukami Best-Sellers Are Now Available

The Lucky Fortune Series

Watch Your Luck Get Better and Better Day By Day! ────────────

Lucky Fortune

This book guides you to better luck and fortune in life. You can learn the four basic principles for getting lucky. By practicing the principles, chanting the Power Call with your eyes on a special logo mark, praying to the gods of celestial bodies as well, you can enjoy fantastic fortune in every aspect of your life!

BY TOSHU FUKAMI

¥1,500 (tax included)

Happiness is Calling You – an Introduction to Japanese Spiritualism! ──────

Divine Order

This book reveals some deep aspects of the origins of fortune. You will surely recognize the importance of understanding the essentials of the spirits and gods in order to acquire heavenly fortune.

BY TOSHU FUKAMI

¥1,500 (tax included)

大 金 運（英語版）

平成4年 3 月 25 日　初　版
平成8年11月10日　第2版

著者	深 見 東 州
翻訳者	ジョン・J・キャロル
発行人	秋 村 泰 造
発行所	株式会社たちばな出版

〒167 東京都杉並区西荻北 3‐42‐19 第6フロントビル
Tel. 03 (5310) 2131
Fax. 03 (3397) 9295

印刷・製本　　錦明印刷株式会社

落丁本・乱丁本はたちばな出版販売部宛にお送り下さい。送料小社負担にてお取り替えいたします。

650.1   Fukami, Toshu
FUKAMI   Let heaven make your
        fortune.

$15.00

MONROE LIBRARY
MONROE, CONNECTICUT

3/97